England's Hideaways

England's Hideaways

Discovering Enchanting Rooms, Stately Manor Houses, and Country Cottages

Meg Nolan van Reesema

PHOTOGRAPHS BY TIM CLINCH

RIZZOLI
NEW YORK

Scotland

England

Nottingham○

○Haworth

London ○

○Dorchester

14

12, 13   16   15

17

18

19

11

10

30   29

9

7, 8   6

5

24–28

23

22   21

1

2

3

4

north

CONTENTS

FRONTISPIECE Augill Castle's fairy-tale façade OVERLEAF A walking path along the Lake District's Sharrow Bay

FOREWORD

In a country where bucolic landscapes and small local inns are the national signature, selecting thirty tucked-away properties in England may seem like fishing in a stocked pond. However, the selection compiled in Meg Nolan van Reesema's third Hideaways book shows sharp and careful scrutiny. By basing her inclusions on the properties' interior décor, Nolan van Reesema celebrates one of England's greatest and age-old assets, interior design.

Our legacy has withstood cheap imitations and contemporary cheekiness and is still heralded for timeless, carved-wood furniture, sumptuous textiles, refined crystal, and hand-painted wallpapers as well as the inherent quirkiness of the way we mix and match styles, colours, and materials unlike any other culture. Some of what we use is imported, allowing us to incorporate and borrow the best from others as suits our climate and culture.

As a designer, I find myself utilizing traditional English design motifs more often than not, and even if not directly, then the inspiration is evident.

Our design heritage should be an enduring source of pride as well as a creative treasury. Just a few years ago England was chastised for being disinterested in design; fortunately the selection here proves the opposite by highlighting the variety of options in our small island country.

I am pleased to have both my properties, Tresanton and Endsleigh, included here and hope their distinct design aesthetics, along with the others in the book, will encourage awareness of England's prettier hotels.

Come and visit and see for yourself.

Olga Polizzi
June 2010

PAGES VI–VII A walking path along the Lake District's Sharrow Bay
OPPOSITE The soft palette of the master suite at Endsleigh House

INTRODUCTION

*T*he opportunity to visit England's tucked-away retreats and evaluate them based on their décor, secluded atmosphere, and overall distinctiveness seemed rather pleasant at the outset. However, once the tour de force began—six weeks of photographing fifty plus properties scattered across the country—the awesome quantity of worthy properties became overwhelming, and I was struck by the magnitude of England's prevailing design style and, moreover, the favorable reaction it caused.

After just a few days of shooting, I recognized that English style is in fact quite a prolific design aesthetic. There was an undeniable familiarity to many of the interiors we found, making it all the more difficult to choose those that merit distinction. I found myself developing a particular fondness for the interiors that evoked houses I have known growing up in Connecticut. I couldn't help but embrace the familiar texture of the fabrics, the traditional color schemes, and the eclectic mix of antique furnishings and finds. I found myself wonderfully soothed by the comfort this style brought. (You'll find that the soothing sensation is rather constant in the book's selected properties.)

Long heralded for its interior design and antique oak, walnut, and mahogany furniture, England enjoys a lauded reputation among designers favoring a classic, traditional style. Having spawned monikers such as "quintessentially English" and sought-after home décor themes like "English Country," "British Colonial," and "English Manor," England's design prowess is evident along with its ability to adapt through the ages. From the floral wallpapers and beloved chintz to the gleaming walnut furnishings of Queen Anne and oak-paneled walls of the Tudor reign, English design has not only existed since the beginning of time but has also withstood the test of it. I believe the country's recipe for success is its ability to evolve and stay fresh and sophisticated while maintaining a strong sentiment of home.

My first trip to England was at the young age of eleven. During a visit to the stunning seventeenth-century country manor house in West Sussex known as Drovers, which belonged to my friend Christina Johnson O'Keeffe's mother, Nicola Grover

The beloved croquet lawn
at Chewton Glen

ABOVE The updated interiors at Chewton Glen featuring fabrics by Zoffany and Sanderson
OPPOSITE The ivy-covered side terrace at Chewton Glen—popular for tea and cocktails overlooking the croquet games

Johnson, I experienced a twofold sensation of awe and familiarity. It was as if my childhood fantasies (spurred by Louisa May Alcott, of course) had suddenly appeared in real form. I can still recall how easily I felt comfortable among the estate's grand dimensions and manicured grounds despite never before having set foot in a place of such stature. Today, I am confident this extraordinary reaction was due to the house's tradi-

tional English décor, featuring an artful mix of antiques, fine silk fabrics, elegant upholstery, and such fanciful items as a zebra-skin rug.

Fortunately, in many of England's smaller hotels this phenomenon of simultaneous comfort and enchantment is not lost. Perhaps the two best examples are the beloved and iconic properties Blakes in London and Chewton Glen on the edge of the New Forest. Given

their enormous popularity and celebrated recognition, I could hardly include them as "hideaways," yet I could hardly ignore them. With its decadent, over-the-top décor, Blakes has been touted as one of the first "fashionable small hotels." Draping fine fabrics over the beds and lavishing pillows, throw rugs, and uniquely textured furnishings throughout the guest rooms, designer Anouska Hempel created a calming and

OPPOSITE Anouska Hempel's signature pillow-laden bed
ABOVE Blakes' discreet Chelsea façade, and one of its more subdued, though ever-elegant guest rooms

enthralling oasis from the city. Chewton Glen, a magnificent country house hotel set amid 130 acres of Hampshire countryside—and a member of the esteemed Relais & Châteaux properties—accomplishes a similar feat through its impressive grounds, elegant spa, and captivating yet homey common rooms.

It is this distinct, almost national directive of designing a homelike interior that I believe makes England such a favorable destination for travelers. The idea that a setting, regardless of its formality, is intended to comfort its guests and allow them to absorb the surroundings rather than be overwhelmed by them is remarkably widespread among the great manor houses and country cottages of England. Elegant yet approachable, English design has proven its forti-tude, continuing to inspire reproductions and modern adaptations all around the world. Similarly, I hope the following pages will encourage you to discover your own adaptation of English design.

MEG NOLAN VAN REESEMA
October 2010

HOTEL TRESANTON ST. MAWES, TRURO, CORNWALL

In KEEPING WITH most sought-after destinations, arriving at St. Mawes, the lovely seaside village on the southern, Cornish coast, requires careful navigation and the threat of a few scrapes (to your car, that is) along the way. Known for its winding, thick country lanes, family-friendly beaches, and miles of walking trails in the moors and along the sea, the Cornish coast is a very popular beach getaway, and as a result, hotels, inns, and pubs are in abundance, though few as lauded or as charming as Olga Polizzi's Tresanton in St. Mawes. The village's dramatic gateway, St. Mawes Castle, one of Henry VIII's coastal fortresses, sets the stage for the picturesque hamlet with its glittery bay, typically filled with the criss-crossing of sailboats (St. Mawes even has its own one-design fleet). Roll down the car windows and inhale the salty sea air as you follow the main road down to the white-washed façade of Tresanton. Nevermind the hotel's narrow Main Street entrance and steep hillside setting—two dapper men will rush to meet your car, eagerly relieving you of your keys and promising to deliver your luggage directly to your room. As you enter through the front stone wall, traversing through the skinny whitewashed tunnel entrance, passing a tiny cavernous bar and a brightly striped lounge, then climbing up a narrow stone staircase, you'll wonder whether Greece wasn't the source of inspiration. However, once you've emerged on the hotel's flat deck, its official first level, a massive pot of lavender, boxes of blooming white azaleas and potted palms, and the view

of St. Mawes's quaint, wooden boat-filled harbor reminds you you're still in England. In June, tall white masts and small sailboats with colored sails fill the natural harbor, creating a picturesque scene against the rolling green hillside bluff and the opposing point's ancient lighthouse (whose image is, incidentally, the tasteful logo of Tresanton found embroidered on towels and napkins). Decorated by owner Olga Polizzi, the lauded interior designer behind the luxury hotel collection of her brother, Sir Rocco Forte, Tresanton is recognized as one of the first boutique properties on England's southern coast and enjoys a glamorous reputation as the forbearer in the surrounding area. Olga's decorative prowess and fresh, Mediterranean style was behind Tresanton's substantial, initial buzz and is no doubt responsible for its continuing popularity.

Just behind the umbrella-laden deck is the deceptively spacious ground floor of Tresanton, which includes a small check-in area, a light-filled sitting room, the marina-styled restaurant, and a multipurpose room known as the theater, with a pull-down screen and blue and white mosaic floor that further recalls the Mediterranean. Featuring sets of French doors that open out to the deck and multiple brushed-cotton-covered couches and deep-set armchairs alongside reading lamps and backgammon boards, the sitting room is the clear spot for reposing indoors while still appreciating the seaside breeze or, alternatively, the spot to nestle with a book, safely shut against the English elements and lapping up the warmth from the room's captivating stone

fireplace. Painted an inviting sunny yellow and adorned with a mélange of attractive seascape oil paintings, classic art sculptures, antique side tables and chairs and vases of fresh flowers, the sitting room is inviting regardless of the season—a tribute to the unobtrusive and soothing design style of Ms. Polizzi.

The simple elegance of Tresanton carries from the design through to the food and dining experience. The multiwindowed wood-paneled restaurant is decorated in a harborside-appropriate palette of crisp navy blues and whites and offers alfresco dining on the two-tiered deck, which is equipped with heat lamps for cooler evenings. Overlooking the ever-engaging harbor, a three-course dinner is deliciously romantic and deserving of a celebratory occasion with tempting dishes like fresh lobster linguine and a savory John Dory with mussels, both perfectly paired with the house Sancerre rosé. Equally scenic and scrumptious, breakfast features a European-style buffet of cereals, fresh fruits, yogurts, and made-to-order hot items while lunch offers seafood fare, both served on the deck shielded from the sun by the blue market umbrellas with spectator-worthy views of the area's frequent sailboat regattas.

Fortunately, despite the hotel's consistent bookings, the pastel village of St. Mawes remains every bit the authentic, sea-beaten English village complete with a rambling pub and fish-and-chips shack. I highly recommend taking the easy downhill stroll along the main seafront street (daily, even) to check out the village's colorful stone cottages, various small shops (including Onda, owned by

Olga's fashion-savvy daughter), wooden-table cafés, and my favorite, The Jolly Sailor's Takeaway, where a cold beer and fish and chips are readily available from the corner doorway counter. Then stop at the natural harbor's wide mouth, where an elevated grassy park with wooden benches and hydrangea bushes offers the picture-perfect vista of the simple serenity of summer on the Cornish coast.

For a more intimate and exhilarating experience with the sea—and one only available to guests at the Tresanton—hop aboard the hotel's gorgeous, eight-meter classic yacht, *Penuccia*. Originally owned by the Rizzoli family, Penuccia now moors just in front of Tresanton and is skippered by Tresanton's delightful young captain, Jamie. Available for either a morning or afternoon sail, depending on conditions, *Penuccia* offers a privileged perspective of the area, particularly for classic yacht lovers.

ROOMS

Given the main structure's considerable age and the hotel's overall hillside architecture, the twenty-nine rooms at Tresanton vary dramatically in size and layout. Divided among the main house, an old English stone structure with lead-frame windows and wooden shutters, and the more modern wooden building tucked into the hillside above the main house (and requiring more stairs), along with the Nook, a tangential two-bedroom cottage, recently renovated with its own private terrace with access down to the sea, and the upcoming three-bedroom Rock Cottage, each of the rooms at Tresanton is individually decorated with local Cornish art and antiques personally collected by Ms. Polizzi. The rooms in the main house are particularly crisp and clean,

with sisal carpet, linen-covered sleigh beds (a signature of Ms. Polizzi), and framed architectural or floral prints, while the rooms at the top, or Upper Tresanton, as it's known (numbers 22–27), are best suited for families, each featuring two bedrooms, a living room, and a spacious balcony staring out to sea. All of the rooms offer sea views, and moreover, convey Polizzi's penchant for simple, classic décor with neutral palettes, thick, bold stripes on the curtains or throw blankets and pillows, and traditional wainscoting and marble or tile floors in the bathrooms. The bedding, a particular consideration of Ms. Polizzi, features freshly pressed white percale coverlets, king-size goose-down pillows, and striped wool blankets folded at the foot of each bed. The minimal furnishings—a varying ensemble including a small writer's desk, an antique bureau or armoire, plus a twill-covered armchair or rattan chaise—ensure the room's overarching simplicity and fresh appeal—particularly when the windows are thrown open to the sea breeze. Attractive details like embroidered linen laundry bags, bedside crystal water carafes, and antique novels complete the relaxed and homey environment of the room—making it easy to tuck in early at night and stay in bed in the morning. However, it's worth noting that the seagulls begin their hunt very early in the morning, along with the sunrise. It's best to shut the curtains and, if you can bear it, the windows too. Despite the larger size and privacy enhancements of the Nook and the family-style rooms and even the roomier, second-floor rooms of the main house (numbers 1–13), I found myself preferring the tight dimensions and somewhat odd configurations of the cozy, third floor rooms of the main building. Tucked into the sloping eaves

of the tiled roof with direct sea views glimpsed through lead-framed picture windows with linen curtains that sincerely billow in the sea breeze, the attic-style rooms (numbers 13–21) better suit the presumed setting for a romantic hideaway along the moody Cornish coast. Room 19, with its butter-yellow walls and brown striped accents on the blanket, struck just the right balance of worn-in comfort within a freshly appointed guest room, similarly with Room 16's palette of fern green and cream. Of course, if you simply can't stand tripping over one another and require sufficient closet space (the dimensions do verge on cramped) and roomy bathrooms, I suggest you head down to Rooms 1 or 2. Or if you want more furnishings and spots to drape yourself, then check out Room 6 or especially 7, whose cushioned window seat is a bonus during both sunny and rainy days.

The mood at Tresanton is one of tranquility—though families are quite welcome, encouraged even with kid-themed movie nights and special family-designed rooms. Nevertheless, guests are primed to relax, with ample cushioned lounge chairs both inside and out and a continuous bar service throughout the day. Beware that this can mean some guests never leave, and I admit, I found myself wishing that some stalwart loungers on the main deck would take themselves (and their bathing getups) to the neighboring beach; luckily there are plenty of places to repose. And when all else fails, you can always head out for a sail, or order another glass of that satiating rosé.

AUTHOR'S NOTE The hotel is currently building a separate three-bedroom building, featuring its own garden, kitchen, and living room.

ABOVE The Union Jack waves proudly in the constant breeze OPPOSITE, CLOCKWISE FROM TOP Olga Polizzi's signature bold prints on the bed; Tresanton's classic yacht, *Penuccia*; Tresanton's branded water bottles in the guest rooms

THE COVE LAMORNA, NEAR PENZANCE, CORNWALL

Tucked into the thick green hillside alongside a rippling creek with a rolling valley view down to a rocky seaside inlet, the Cove, aptly named, offers a modern hideaway of apartment-style accommodations favored by families and contemporary-minded couples. Overwhelmed with aqua accents—from the surfboard outside the front door to the furnishings in the small bar—the original stone and clapboard building has been remodeled into fifteen separate, self-catering apartments, also available as hotel residences, adding contemporary concept and flair to an otherwise sleepy hamlet in Cornwall.

A good twenty minutes past Penzance, on the southern coast of Cornwall, the Cove, like most true hideaways, is not easily accessible. One must trudge up hills, swerve alongside bushes, and pass under heavy tree canopies to reach its striking aqua signage and eventual entrance. As you descend down the tight driveway past the historic façade of the building, complete with a rooftop bell, at first glance the hotel appears as traditional as the neighboring stone cottages. (In fact, the Cove was once a chapel and temperance hotel and was later owned by Churchill's friend Sir Alfred James Munnings, the painter and former president of the Royal Academy of Arts in London.) However, upon entering the reception area, with its sleek, curved desk and glittering metallic chandelier, the traditional look evaporates and the cool modernity begins. Continuing down the main hall past aqua pots of cascading lilies, you'll find the peanut-shaped pool, stone patio, and sparkling views down through the valley out to the churning sea. The pool is not only the epicenter of action (particularly for children) but also was the inspiration behind the saturated turquoise color scheme of the hotel. Just behind the pool's glass-enclosed deck is an alluring grassy path leading down to the cove. I highly recommend following the path down to the sea, then heading to the left, all the way to the end of the first rocky point—the views and crashing waves are just what you'd expect from the foreboding English sea. If you're ambitious, the walk continues around the other side of the bend and leads to a small fishing village, ideal for a serving of local fare or an afternoon pint. This walk, in fact, is part of the beloved "Western Walk" that stretches along the majority of the Cornish coast. However long you choose to hike, the views are guaranteed to impress, while the sea's crashing symphony will propel you onward.

During the summer and fall months the Cove also offers photography and cooking classes, including one focusing on the food harvested from the neighboring gardens. For adventurers, there's some great surfing nearby, and the Cove has a special relationship with Cornwall's Southern Surf School. With plans for expansion and current in-room spa facilities, the Cove has a bright (and surely aqua-tinged) future.

ROOMS

With standard mod-square side tables, ultrasuede bed frames, and matching lampshades, the sixteen one- and two-bedroom apartments possess the same stylized, contemporary décor as the rest of the hotel. Aqua accents abound, from the sitting room's deep couch to the velvet bed pillows and glass lamps. Taupe sisal or cotton weave carpets cover the bedrooms, while polished oak floors run through the sitting room and alcove kitchen. The rooms are fully equipped with four-top electric stoves, ovens, Electrolux dishwashers, remarkably sleek-looking Russell Hobbs toasters, microwaves, washing machines, mini-fridges stocked with water, milk, jams, and butter (which are meant to accompany the fresh bread in the morning and stocked cereals in the cupboards), and the requisite coffee and tea makers. The kitchen, like the hotel itself, has that modified Philippe Starck, minimalistic London loft look, with white granite countertops, graphite cupboards, and chrome appliances. In fact, it is so polished that it resembles a store-model kitchen. In the spacious sitting rooms are deep linen couches facing wall-mounted flat-screen televisions. The large glass desk with a WiFi dock is made more stylish with a Lucite desk chair. The walls are a crisp, white-cotton color and left relatively bare, aside from the one framed boat print above the desk, a kitchen clock, the two TVs (there is also one in the bedroom), and small beach landscape photographs of Tarifa, Spain, taken by a Spanish friend of the owners. The adornments (clay vases, leather directory, and Venetian window shades), similarly in aqua tones, stand out enthusiastically, though ring a bit like props. The addition of some fresh flowers in

PAGE 12 The canyonlike view down to the sea OPPOSITE The Cove's popular platform pool and inspiration behind the property's color scheme ABOVE The mixture of the traditional and modern architecture; an unmistakable marketing prop for the property's surf camp

the vases and some more indigenous curio (read authentic) would go a long way. Room 10 offers a particularly stunning view from the bedroom, which gazes out over the pool directly down the valley chute toward the cove. It's a bit higher up than the sea-view rooms below, meaning pool noise is less bothersome. The queen-size bed is firm and cozy, with ample firm pillows. Nine apartments have sea views, and the majority of them sleep up to four people. They differ in size, so it's best to ask for details when booking, especially the number of bathrooms. Apartments 15 and 16 are newer than the others and have separate entrances plus spacious balconies, larger kitchens, and two complete bedrooms plus a pullout couch.

The room style is clearly well suited to families, but the bathrooms don't have bathtubs—a seeming blasphemy for an English hotel. The showers, however, are roomy and have rain showerheads, and in Room 10 there's a big window with a treetop view of the valley.

Overall the rooms are simple and functional if not particularly inspired, although you will find that after running in from the frequent rain, the cozy, aquamarine-themed décor mixed with recessed lighting, fluffy white duvets, and LCD TVs comfortably positioned opposite the beds make the damp weather feel very far away. More recently, the rooms have become available to guests on a membership/part-own-

ership level through the newly established Cove Club. Opened in 2006, the Cove sought to deliver updated, self-sufficient accommodations with a "bit more style" to the new wave of young Cornwall visitors. However, if you're yearning for a bit of the old-fashioned, the neighboring pub, the Winking Lamona, just down the hill, offers the more presumed English countryside ambiance. I'm willing to bet, though, once you've taken the requisite walk through the Cove's surrounding gardens and along the rocky coastline, the property's London-mod style—or "chic seaside," as owner Lee Magner puts it—may be the exact contrast you crave.

OPPOSITE, CLOCKWISE FROM TOP LEFT Simple furnishings in the guestrooms; the lush surroundings; the bar's aqua-stained glass top and complimentary cookies; a guestroom's bright sitting room with pull-out couch ABOVE The light-filled alcove off the bar

WHITEHOUSE CHILLINGTON, DEVON

ARRIVING FOR THE FIRST TIME at Whitehouse can prove a bit tricky given the lack of signage and the sharp turnoff from the main road. However, once you have found it you may wonder how you could have ever missed it. Sitting at the top of the main road in the small hamlet of Chillington, near Kingsbridge in South Devon, Whitehouse is a clear outlier in its neighborhood, showcasing what's to come in relatively sleepy South Devon by offering an updated style of design-centric hospitality alongside incredibly great food.

The classic Georgian-style stone house with white trim and attractive crawling ivy dates back to 1860 and presents an original of an oft-copied architectural style. (New England is crawling with replicas.) Curiously enough, during World War II the town of Chillington was evacuated, and American GIs occupied Whitehouse, perhaps taking the blueprints for the beloved home design with them.

With corner urns on the roof, a long lawn (begging for croquet), a well-manicured garden, and a sizable terrace furnished with Dedon wicker furniture under white market umbrellas, the exterior presents a traditional face on a purposefully untraditional interior. More of an upscale B&B (with sleek, en suite bathrooms) than a boutique hotel, Whitehouse offers an intimate and personal atmosphere.

Run by Tamara, Ally, and Matthew—friends from university with hospitality and/or culinary backgrounds—the property features an eclectic mix of contemporary décor and is run with vibrant enthusiasm that's palpable upon entry. Tamara, the bubbly personality of the trio, is the driving force behind both the funky interior design and the eager service delivery. It's due to the careful sourcing and cataloguing of elements from her travels that give each room a spark of individuality.

The ground floor of the house includes a study with a welcoming lit fireplace, a cozy sitting room with cracked leather sofas overlooking the yard, and a front meeting room with a single cut-wood table and handsome leather chairs imported from Australia—easily my favorite pieces in the house. Smack in the center is a tiny house bar that serves drinks and snacks at the counter all day long and is the natural coffeehouse, collecting guests with their computers lounging over coffee. The main attraction, though, is the conservatory-style dining room that seats up to thirty-five people and is children-free after 6 p.m., ensuring a more serene culinary affair. The dining room is festively lit with fluorescent-colored votives and a large crystal chandelier hanging in the center of the room. Mismatched wood and leather seating give it a funky and casual ambiance, while the tableware is colorful and varying. The food, prepared by the very talented Ally, is simply phenomenal. Everything from the lamb chops to the scallops to the poached egg in the morning was served to the highest standards utilizing the freshest ingredients Ally can find. Caught in the local craze, Ally sources all her own meats and vegetables from local purveyors and is known to affect prices with her discerning eye.

South Devon, or the South Hams, as the area is known, is renowned for its small grassy lanes and coastal footpaths, not to mention abundant pubs. The hotel has a couple of bicycles for loan and will happily arrange a picnic to bring along. Neighboring beaches offer all possible wind sports plus surfing and sea kayaking. The hotel also offers a complimentary membership to the Dart Marina Spa in nearby Dartmouth, where you can use the pool, steam room, and gym, or book a treatment. In-room massages are also available with advanced booking, though it's best to do this only if you are staying in one of the larger suite-style rooms. A rare and very appreciated amenity is offered by the local taxi, which allows fares to be charged right to your room—ideal after an evening pub crawl. And while some of the older gentry may shrug at the idea of a worthwhile hideaway down in South Devon, the movers and shakers of contemporary England seem to smell the fresh appeal and are arriving in droves.

ROOMS

The five rooms at Whitehouse are similarly styled with modern touches (arc lamps, Kartell desk chairs) and kitschy notes (metallic wallpaper, purple velvet armchairs, bucket swings, and Fatboy bean bags), though they differ in configuration and size. The largest, Room 5, has an enormous bathroom with walk-in shower and center-court tub, plus separate wood basin vanities. The newest, Room 6, up in the attic, is quite cozy and has a surprisingly tall and spacious

PAGE 18 The cozy, vintage-inspired look of the Whitehouse drawing room ABOVE The Georgian-style exterior masks the contemporary eclectic décor inside OPPOSITE The inviting oak-incased shower and tub in guest room 1

shower featuring a sauté-pan-sized shower-head. Room 4 has an endearing cow-and-goat-patterned wallpaper and cow-fur ottoman at the food of the bed, while Room 3 has perhaps the most massive bed in Devon if not southern England. Custom-made by a local craftsman, the wood-framed king-plus-size bed has an inviting fluffy white duvet and hordes of starched white pillows. Room 1 is my favorite, with a natural-toned twig-and-branch wallpaper motif and a striking wood-paneled sunken shower. It's exactly my kind of showering-in-the-woods-experience. Plus the room

faces the back, which makes it immune to the road noise that afflicts Rooms 3, 4, and 5. With only six rooms, Whitehouse is often rented as an entire property, as it is an ideal spot for a group trip or small weddings. Then again, since the rooms are so wonderfully equipped (Nespresso makers, large wall-mounted flat-screen TVs, enormous beds with Frette linens, and roll-top tubs), a romantic mini-holiday here is perhaps even more superlative.

On yet another creative and entrepreneurial note, Whitehouse has its own line of bath and skin products. The 100 percent veg-

etarian and vegan hand-blended concoctions range from damask rose to peppermint and come in recyclable packaging. The products are available at the hotel or can be ordered online. The conditioner is my favorite, along with the silky face cream that is left on your pillow at turndown. Another quirky element, and one that Tamara admittedly borrowed from another hotel, are the cooler minibars, custom wood boxes that open from the top to reveal a selection of complimentary milk, water, wine, Champagne, and sodas.

ABOVE A refreshing spot for a spot of tea OPPOSITE, CLOCKWISE FROM TOP LEFT The beloved poached egg breakfast; a Dutch-inspired fireplace; perhaps one of the largest beds in southern England; chinoiserie wallpaper and silk-covered chairs in one of the guest rooms

*R*IGHT ON THE border of Cornwall and Devon counties, Hotel Endsleigh sits on an impressive 250 acres of luscious gardens, with vistas of the rolling Dartmoor hills and towering redwood trees that were planted specifically to remind the original owner, Georgiana, Duchess of Bedford, of her beloved Scotland. In the early nineteenth century, the duchess lived at Endsleigh with her three stepsons, while the duke came and went, spending most of his days onsite fishing on the property's river access. In 1814 the duchess hired the celebrated landscape designer Humphry Repton to design the massive surrounding gardens. His results are nothing short of masterful. He is responsible for the fascinating arboretum that towers behind the house, the broad terraces that pitch down to the teeming river below, and the multitudes of rhododendrons, ceanothis, and violets that pervade the planted flower gardens.

Designed by Sir Jeffry Wyatville, renowned for remodeling Windsor Castle, the historic 1810 Endsleigh House was built in the style known as *cottage orné*. Despite the duke's intent for the property to be a simple spot where he and his family could escape their formal life and enjoy the countryside, the house is hardly simple, boasting an entire servants' wing, sixteen guest rooms (the duke's was even outfitted with a miniature chapel), vast kitchens, and a curious back sun terrace supported by tree-trunk columns and the ground inlaid with sheep's knuckles.

Overlooking the Tamor River, famous for both its exclusivity and enviable salmon population, Hotel Endsleigh was for a time a prestigious fishing club open from May to October and available in the winter months for hunting parties. In the late 1980s the club formed a charitable trust of the gardens and has been welcoming outside guests to walk the surrounding scenery, bringing in revenue for some initial renovations to the house.

Since 2005 the property has been under the elegant command of English interior designer (and owner of Cornwall's Hotel Tresanton) Olga Polizzi and her daughter, Alex. Upon purchasing the Grade I–listed property and its gardens, Polizzi and her daughter were forced to contend with considerable setbacks like dry rot, no heating system, insufficient water and gas, and broken windows. Nevertheless, it took just one year for the two to restore the lauded Regency house to its original refinement while carefully preserving its rustic country home personality (along with the crowd-pleasing move of returning the fishing-club rights to the ten directors). The quick turnaround is somewhat miraculous given the amount of work that was done: adding cast-iron radiators for heat; installing new water, gas, and electricity lines; digging a new cesspit; refurbishing all sixteen of the guest bathrooms; and building a fire escape from the second floor. As Polizzi says, "You name it, we've done it." The interiors also posed quite a challenge. When Polizzi bought the house, only a few furnishings and a few of the listed wallpapers were included. Although the duke's original furnishings were made available to Polizzi for purchase, this wise daughter of a successful hotelier chose instead to stick to her budget and select only one or two pieces plus a few plaster statuettes. Everything else was later auctioned off by Christie's, raising nearly £650,000.

Today, Hotel Endsleigh feels and looks every bit as classic and prestigious as it undoubtedly once was. The austerity of the property is evident immediately upon entering the foyer, whose polished faux-wood-paneled, trompe l'oeil painted walls, solid rosewood table, and enormous antique map of the Ordinance of Devon County mark the impressive origins of the house. Throughout the first floor, which was in far better shape than the upstairs at the time of purchase, washed-out primary colors cling to the walls, while the hodgepodge of antique furnishings collected on Polizzi's various shopping trips give the house a lived-in sense of comfort. In the main living room, a rainbow-striped ottoman claims center stage, while brown and green velvet, curved-back chairs with plush seat pillows and classic two-toned ticking bring a stylish touch to the room's typical country-English sophistication. Polizzi's signature stripes dominate the décor and appear exceptionally attractive on two French settees in the sitting room. The walls range from wood paneled to mint green to the occasional wallpaper, while the dining room's tall leaded windows overlooking the garden feature original artwork of the duke's friends' family crests. In fact, so fastidious in her decorating is Polizzi that she rearranges the furniture every year just

to make sure returning guests enjoy an updated, fresh feel.

Furthermore, details such as the hotel's custom English bone china, hand-painted with leaf motifs of the trees and plants in the surrounding gardens, and the vintage silver-topped water glasses assure guests that a deft and elegant hand is steering the ship. Perhaps the most impressive detail, however, are the three hundred votives placed all over the hotel's massive ground floor and lit every night to create a truly dramatic atmosphere. The votive colors range from deep purple to silver to red at Christmastime. Their overall effect on the hotel's narrow hallways and numerous sitting rooms is remarkably warming.

Endsleigh's magnificent setting is meant to be enjoyed at a delightfully calm pace, whether it's high tea taken in the violet-filled children's garden or at a picnic specially prepared by staff; the intent is to be languid. However, there is one rather active pursuit that is a requisite: an afternoon fly-fishing session on the illustrious River Tamor. The hotel's resident gillie, John Dennis, formerly of England's eminent Test River, where he was a frequent guide to the royal family, will happily escort you through the property's multiple wading pools and gaily share with you the history of the house and, if prodded, amusing details from fly-fishing with England's upper gentry.

ROOMS

As one would hope of a country mansion amid flowering gardens, the sixteen guest rooms at Endsleigh are all abloom with floral accents and cheery colors. Thoughtfully furnished and decorated by Olga, who saw to it that each room's antique elements, such as crown molding, leaded windows, and marble mantels, were highlighted, the rooms offer individual character, creating favorites among guests. Admittedly, Polizzi went "a bit flowery," using Bernard Thorpe materials with a lot of muted fabrics in the décor. Her choices were influenced by the gardens, featuring multiple greens and Regency colors like bright blues and yellow. Of course, given the house's historic origins, the rooms vary tremendously in size and layout. As Helen, the charming Master of House, must frequently explain to inquirers, "We don't really have standard rooms." Rooms 5 and 8 feature the exquisite original, listed wallpaper and are oft-requested given the rarity of

sleeping amid such historic walls. In both rooms, Polizzi offsets the celebrated paper with neutral tones and one chosen color pulled from the wallpaper's design, which she lavishes on the upholstery on the headboard, side chair, and elegant suede curtains. Wisely, she laid down bordered sisal carpets over the old floors to give the rooms an updated feel and outfitted the beds with embroidered Frette linens featuring a delicate E on each pillow.

Room 1 is the most requested room of the house. The only room on the ground floor, it has very tall ceilings, French doors that open right onto the side garden, a small sitting room, an enormous bathroom, and delicate antique linens. The bed is deliciously comfortable and it's hard not to imagine oneself as a celebrated guest of the duke while drifting off to sleep. Many of the rooms feature massive, linen-covered sleigh beds—another Polizzi touch—which set an impressive tone (in so much as they are not four-poster beds) and keep the guest snug and content. The bathrooms also differ widely from room to room, and one should be sure to request a shower if needed. They all are recently refurbished with marble or mosaic tile and England's Lefroy and Brooks fixtures. To my delight, similar to Tresanton, Endsleigh also provides darling embroidered laundry bags hanging from the wall. Of all the rooms, Room 8 is my favorite. Not only is the wallpaper the most beautiful, with its garden design featuring peacocks, butterflies, and lovely orange flowers, but the soft gray French wingback chair, cozy cream blanket, and mini stone terrace with a direct view down the garden wall make it the most enchanting room in the house—and particularly alluring on a rainy day.

10 GEORGE STREET   YORK

*T*UCKED WITHIN A monotonous line of Georgian brick town houses on York's infamous George Street (the notorious highwayman Dick Turpin, who was tried and hanged in York in 1739, is buried just around the corner), Number Ten would be indiscernible if it weren't for the blooming window box and bright aqua trim on the windowsills and front door. Just as its brightly painted front door suggests, the three-bedroom 10 George Street strikes a remarkable contrast to its neighbors, featuring a mixed bag of eccentric décor ranging from camp to Gothic to surprisingly traditional and offering a memorable self-catering option in York.

Stepping across the threshold into 10 George Street instantly reminds the guest of the risk imposed by staying somewhere nontraditional, while the eye-catching interior of the house (decorative eggs, Chinese porcelain teapots, and handcrafted ivory and whalebone ships) conveys the unexpected reward. Reminiscent of a Harry Potter set, the house's mishmash of styles, from traditional Tudor paneling in the lounge to Victorian iron mannequins in the deluxe bedroom, and personable elements like hand-painted signs on the doors and a reading tray for the bathtub, with special holders for wineglasses and candles, keep guests guessing at what they will happen upon next. Decorated by owner Heather Robinson, who ran her own interior design business until 2000 and has always loved anything "theatrical or over the top," 10 George Street is filled with thrift-shop finds and a purposefully uncoordinated, eye-catching

look. According to Robinson, she sought to create a distinct place, full of the weird and wonderful. The second-floor bathroom is her favorite room, tickled by her own idea of setting a tub in a bookcase.

The lounge is easily the most conventional room, with a masculine appeal that features oak paneling and floors, inlaid bookshelves, cushy leather sofas, amber-colored ceiling, an open fireplace, and a flat-screen TV with DVD player. Tucked between the galley kitchen (which is small though fully stocked and functional) is the Gothic-style dining room with ornamental chairs and a mahogany table fittingly strewn with candles. The most appealing aspect is the small back garden, accessed from the dining area through the French doors, which flood the ground floor with light and offer a quaint, topiary-filled view. The garden also features a table and chairs ideal for alfresco meals (for two) or lingering over coffee and tea. Up the narrow staircase, richly wallpapered in the whimsical design Trade Cards by Lewis & Wood, you'll find the deluxe guest room, twin room, and main bathroom. (Note that there is no bathroom on the ground floor and so climbing the tight staircase is a multiple-times-a-day affair). In accordance with Robinson, I found the main bathroom to be the highlight of the second floor, with its decadent wood-paneled tub sunken between matching bookshelves, French console sink, and walk-in shower. I made sure to follow the brochure's suggestion and ran a bubble bath, lit the provided tub-side candles, and enjoyed my book till my toes

pruned. The library setting is rather tempting and pleasurable, particularly for someone like me who has been wilting the pages of paperbacks with tub steam for years. Given the narrow dimensions of the house and the top two floors devoted to bedrooms—two on the second floor and the master up on the third—the main living space can feel a bit confining, providing the guest all the more reason to go out and explore the city.

Just a five-minute walk from York's famous Shambles (the crooked street and inspiration behind Harry Potter's Diagon Alley) and ten minutes from the soaring York Minster, George Street is ideally situated to enjoy the sites of York on foot. (Fortunately the house comes equipped with a parking spot, allowing you to leave your car out front without any pesky fines.) Located in the medieval Walmgate residential area within the city walls and just a block from foodie favorites Walmgate and Fossgate Streets, 10 George Street provides quick access to various specialty shops, including the Barbakan Delicatessen, which offers such imported goodies as South African biltong; casual bistros such as Melton's Too with tasty, home-cooked fare; and delicious restaurants like Paradiso del Cibo or Blue Bicycle. Given that York is one of England's major cities, visiting 10 George Street should be timed appropriately. I recommend going during the cooler, slightly less touristy months of the fall or winter. Something about the Gothic-style city, with its haunted past and medieval character, makes the

colder months seem more appropriate for enjoying its distinct (and quirky) charm. For Robinson, York is especially magical at Christmastime, with open-air markets, the festival of angels (when ice sculptures line the streets), and beautiful church services at the minster. Fortunately, 10 George Street complies with the owners preference and feels coziest with a fire burning and the various candles lit.

ROOMS

The three-bedroom setup at 10 George Street is perfect for a small family or two couples, maybe one with children (though beware of the steep stairs!). Although there are enough beds for six, the tight dimensions of the old house can quickly make it feel cramped if all six are stuck inside too long; thus, I suggest either a short overall stay or limiting the group to four. Located one flight up, both the deluxe and twin room feature feminine details. The twin room has an original cast-iron fireplace and Cath Kidston linens, while the deluxe guest room offers a king-size bed with a French-inspired bed crown of turquoise raw silk. Unfortunately neither room offers extra seating or much storage space. Despite the somewhat overdramatic Empire style of the deluxe room (damask wallpaper, a Romanesque chandelier, and a fully outfitted Victorian mannequin in the corner), the bed is wonderfully plush and the room enjoys a quiet backyard view, ensuring a sound

night's sleep. The house's pièce de résistance, however is the penthouse-style master bedroom situated on the top floor, up another narrow staircase. Modeled after a lavish opera set, the room is meant to be as sensuous as possible. From the truly massive, carved four-poster bed to the freestanding roll-top bath tucked beneath the vaulted eaves and the eye-popping Renaissance painting, Crivelli's *The Annunciation,* the room is undoubtedly theatrical. Sleeping underneath the carved canopy in the master bedroom among the multiple iridescent silk and velvet pillows is, as promised, a decadent experience, with a Tempurpedic mattress, sateen linens, and, rather surprisingly, a direct view of the flat-screen TV. Given that it's on the top floor, the room can get a bit stuffy and warm during the summer, furthering the case for visiting during the cooler months. Beware, the bathroom in the master bedroom is indeed *in* the bedroom, with an open layout featuring the tub just a few feet from the bed and the toilet and sink tucked around the corner, discreetly out of view from the bed. As I hope is evident, staying at 10 George Street offers a distinct experience best suited for adventurous types willing to immerse themselves in the wackier ways of English design.

AUTHOR'S NOTE For a similar experience in London, visit Forty Winks, David Carter's delightful Queen Anne town house located in the East End (see page 194).

The turquoise entrance sign stands out on the brick-lined street

ABOVE The guestroom's marble-topped sink and damask wallpaper set the dramatic tone   OPPOSITE, CLOCKWISE FROM TOP LEFT The Tudor paneled walls of the front lounge; the Victorian bed style of the deluxe room; the curio-lined mantel of the drawing room; Lewis & Wood's Trade Cards wallpaper

WHATLEY MANOR EASTON GREY, MALMESBURY

THE ENTRANCE OF Whatley Manor is stage-set to perfection, with grand sandstone gateposts, a long, winding driveway lined with lime trees, a drystone wall that took local Cotswold craftsmen two years to build, and surrounding manicured verges stocked with shiny chestnut horses. An indiscreet sign points you down the hill toward the hotel's exterior wall and massive oak doors, which open slowly as your car approaches. Once admitted, you must circle around the traditional courtyard aptly styled with a two-hundred-year old olive tree at its center. In the summer, the circular rows of lavender bushes and white lilies intoxicate the guests with fresh scents, offering one of the better arrivals to a hotel.

Waiting at the manor's front door is Jon, the black-vested porter, ready to open the car door and relieve you of your luggage. It's formal city-style service but in the middle of Wiltshire countryside. The owners' Swiss background may have something to do with the efficiency and precision of the manor's overall presentation. Inside, the pristine glamour continues, with original wood paneling from the late 1850s in the front drawing room and generously sized living room. The oldest part of the house dates back to 1857, and a few wooden doors stand as testament along with the walls, while the majority of the house—floors, banisters, and tangential wings—hails from the 1920s. The attention to preserving the grand history and glamour of Whatley Manor is evident, from the traditional-style interiors featuring eclectic antique furnishings and handsome leather wallpapers to the exceptional gardens. Originally designed by Elizabeth Richardson and now tended by head gardener Barry Holman, the gardens are separated into twenty-six different areas, allowing for hours of meandering and ample secret spots. Each of the planted areas has its own theme, ranging from herbaceous to rose to loggia, and runs alongside a natural grassy meadow, towering woodlands of oak, ash, and hazel trees, and even a mossy riverbank with a Cotswold stone niche. The variety available during a garden walk is simply stupendous. With more than twelve acres of English countryside, just on the border of the ever-popular Cotswolds, Whatley Manor guarantees seclusion and privacy, away from the herds of touring "walkers."

Thanks to the manor's age, it's no surprise that the house maintains a slightly rambling layout, with two staircases, twisting hallways that look confoundedly similar, and some awkwardly squat furniture. However, this only adds to the charm of the main house, while the huge size of the property—a tangential guest wing plus a sprawling stable building that houses a full spa, meeting space, forty-person screening room where weekly movies are shown with dinner, contemporary-style bar, and Swiss-chalet-themed restaurant, Le Mazot—keeps the entire experience feeling spontaneous and almost museumlike. (The donkey statues in the stable yard, a gift from the owner's father, further the visual experience.) The spa area can be accessed either through the central courtyard or, for those less inclined to roam in their robes, via an underground passageway connecting the manor house basement to the stable building, passing the surprisingly well-equipped gym along the way. This is an important feature for those prone to overindulging, particularly since Whatley Manor is an entirely hedonistic affair.

Awarded its second Michelin star in 2009, the Whatley Manor Dining Room and its chef, Martin Burge, are just as much the draw to the manor as anything else. With a bountiful herb garden right outside his kitchen, a dedicated team, and a trusting boss, Burge feels free to create in the kitchen, delivering dishes like veal with hazelnut puree and langoustine tails with cauliflower puree. The tasting menu—four courses with an *amuse-bouche* and pre-dessert—is highly recommended given that the portions are not too large and it tends to be a better showcase of Burge's skill. With wine pairings available from an extensive list, why not indulge when at a two-star Michelin restaurant? Filled with warm light from the mullioned windows overlooking the garden, the Dining Room is pleasantly intimate, with Italian silk fabrics, soft recessed lighting, and just forty seats.

After an evening of culinary triumph, what better way to digest than an afternoon (or day!) at Whatley Manor's Aquarius Spa. As the only La Prairie five-star center outside London, and stocked with talented technicians plus a series of thermal cabins, an indoor/outdoor hydrotherapy pool, and hot stone relaxation loungers, Whatley Manor is a bona fide spa destination.

Regardless of whether you're having a full day of treatments or just a simple facial, the do-not-miss element of the entire spa experience is lounging in the hydrotherapy pool's reflexology jet Jacuzzi and looking out the full-length glass window to the spectacular garden of bluebells and foxgloves. It's a decadent take on the beloved English bath. If all the lounging has you feeing a bit lazy, take out the pair of beautiful Swedish Skeppshult-designed bicycles (serious designer bikes) and wander the area's bushy country lanes or simply pedal the hotel's lengthy driveway. Never fear, the handsome leather-walled bar will be there to greet you upon return with its plush window seats, ideal for an evening cocktail overlooking the gardens.

ROOMS

The twenty-three guest rooms at Whatley Manor are all individually designed, differing significantly in décor and layout, though consistent in their high quality. Ranging from the traditional country English style to the enchanting styles of the Far East, the guest rooms are designed to comfort as much as they are to awe their visitors. Decadently adorned, guest rooms feature designer wallpapers by Brunschwig & Fils and Nina Campbell, and furnishings from the collections of American chair designer John Hutton and France's Forestier. The upholstery fabrics are rich and colorful, hailing from the houses of Rubelli, Canovas, and Nobilis, while one room has suede-covered walls by Chivasso Carlucci. The international representation of décor selections is impressive, particularly for a house so steeped in Swiss tradition (Swiss tapestries adorn the walls along the staircase). On the

OPPOSITE, CLOCKWISE FROM TOP LEFT Rich, crimson colors adorn one guest room; the country-manor-inspired décor in the sitting room; the fresh, tailored look of a guest room; animal prints in another guest room
ABOVE One of the manor's original mid-nineteenth-century banisters; the artfully accessorized bar

other hand, the strikingly modern technology in the rooms (wireless Internet service, flat-screen TVs, and Bang & Olufsen sound systems) and the soundproof walls feel very Swiss indeed. The bathrooms are wonderfully appointed with sunken tubs and walk-in showers stocked with elegant Floris products. Futhermore, most bathrooms have windows, which makes an enormous difference, particularly when combating jet lag. Room 12 evokes the richness of India with a peach and green color scheme, raffia-texture wallpaper, and a pigment-dyed, elephant-

print bedspread and Maharaja-style print on the silk curtains, while Room 8 conjures up Thailand with tiger prints on the bed and curtains and a bamboo-inspired wallpaper, though the four-poster bed and massive Biedermeier armoire keep you rooted in Continental Europe. Despite the vast range in style of décor (making some rooms more appealing than others), all of the guest rooms are exceedingly comfortable. And because they do vary so greatly in their style and look, it's hard to imagine everyone feeling the same about each room, so my sug-

gestion for choosing is to do so according to view—after all, waking up to a view of the grounds will freshen your morning no matter the color of the bedspread. For me, the best view is in Room 10. Though not a suite, Room 10 is quite spacious with a corner layout, decorated in pleasing gold and beige tones with a desk, small sitting area, and grandly positioned king-sized bed. The room's best feature, though, are the two walls of mullioned windows overlooking the herbaceous gardens, Cotswold stone gazebo, and riverbank.

ROYAL CRESCENT HOTEL BATH

$\mathcal{N}$ESTLED IN ONE of Europe's, and certainly England's, most prestigious locations, the Royal Crescent Hotel occupies the two central buildings of Bath's historic eighteenth-century architectural feat, the Crescent. Both built by John Wood Jr., the hotel's two Grade I–listed stone buildings offer the rare and intimate experience of staying in a living monument. Unknown to many tourists, behind the Crescent lie beautiful gardens that date back to the reign of George III. The secluded green sanctuary is at the disposal of guests of the Royal Crescent Hotel for lounging, a game of bowls, afternoon tea, or an alfresco meal. At the back edge of the garden are the former coach houses, now converted into luxury suites, the hotel's expansive spa, and the highly lauded (deservedly so) Dower House restaurant.

Pulling up to the Royal Crescent Hotel offers a distinct, memorable experience. The top-hat-clad doorman swiftly opens the car door, allowing you to step out and enter past the eighteenth-century iron gates into the marble-laid foyer with privileged assurance. The original architecture and historical magnitude of the interior is evident through the soaring ceilings, ceremonial halberds, and imposing marble bust of William Pitt. Despite the austerity of the location, the welcome is warm, with a lit fireplace in the entrance hall, soft Georgian interiors of pale colors, and crystal light features in the main drawing room. The cantilevered Bath stone staircase, yet another vestige of the historic architecture, leads up to the main house guest rooms, captivating visitors with

framed prints, windows overlooking the gardens, and marble busts along the way.

Given Bath's unique hot springs location and spa-themed lineage—from a fifth-century Roman bath site known as Aquae Sulis to the Elizabethan-era spa city to its current status as a World Heritage Site—it is no surprise that the Royal Crescent invested in a full-blown luxury spa and fitness area. Defined by its holistic treatments, teak-lined barrel tubs, indoor pool, and exclusive-brand products, the Bath House Spa features an impressive treatment list, from various body wraps to abundant massage therapies to a full Turkish hammam experience. Booking a day at the spa (it offers an array of one-day retreat programs) is a must.

The hotel's other, modern calling card, particularly to non-guests, is the award-winning Dower House restaurant and its zany head chef, Luke Richards. A meal at the Dower House is imperative during a visit to Bath, with its constantly evolving menu that has influences from the Mediterranean to the Far East. Not only is the food more inventive than at most five-star hotel restaurants and the wine list sincerely varied, but the private, tucked-away garden terrace setting—especially lovely in the spring and summer though equally atmospheric when enclosed in the winter—makes a special occasion truly special. Its contemporary leaf-green-upholstered wingback chairs and grass-design wallpaper offer a striking contrast to the Georgian refinement of the main building and can feel somewhat overwhelming. However, if you request a table by the

windows facing the manicured garden and the elegant back of the historic houses, you'll sink comfortably into the plush seating, satiated by each morsel.

The recipient of multiple awards, including affiliation with Relais & Châteaux, the Royal Crescent Hotel is hardly off the beaten track; in fact, you can't get a more central location in Bath. However, its secret gardens, authentic historical prominence, and elegant period décor mixed with modern amenities make it a top spot to visit when in England, especially if it takes you off your own beaten track.

ROOMS

Despite the building's estimable age, each of the Royal Crescent's forty-five guest rooms and suites feel comfortably light and spacious, with high ceilings, large Georgian windows, and pale color schemes. The soft cream, pink, and blue fabrics and carpeting, typical of eighteenth-century décor, allow the impressive antique furnishings, eighteenth-century portraits, and various ornate details like carved ceilings and mantels to shine through. Surprisingly, the period-style guest rooms all feature handcrafted beds and the requisite modern gadgetry, including flat-screen TVs, DVD players, Wifi, and air-conditioning. The en suite bathrooms are wonderfully updated with powerful showers, plush towels and bathmats, and sizable, double vanities, while the bathrooms in the suites feature roll-top tubs and specially commissioned tiles.

PAGE 43 Bath's famous Crescent ABOVE The delightful back garden at the Royal Crescent Hotel
OPPOSITE Intricate plasterwork carving on the molding and ceiling of the Duke of York suite

Because each room is individually decorated, similar to those at Whatley Manor, it's easier to choose based on view. I recommend a room that faces back toward the impressive gardens and has one of the ample balconies (15, 16, or 38). However, if you're booking a suite, then the Duke of York, overlooking the sward in front of the Crescent, fulfills the desire for prominence. I'm also partial to the Jane Austen and Beau Nash suites located in the separate, seven-bedroom Pavilion area, which provide glorious, light-filled spaces for room service or an afternoon of reading. The Jane Austen's ceiling is a triumph, while the Beau Nash's tangential conservatory leads out to the garden, making it the garden lovers' top choice.

And last, I favor the Lord Nash suite, whose masculine, mahogany-laden décor is softened by the spacious balcony ideal for romance. For the most exclusive spot, try the secluded, four-bedroom Garden Villa. Buried back in the walled, topiary-laden gardens alongside the Dower House restaurant, the former eighteenth-century coach house features its own private garden with stone fountain and three deluxe rooms plus one suite. Ideal for a family or guests seeking ultimate privacy (celebrities with entourages), the Garden Villa provides a botanical sanctuary alongside five-star amenities and services at your own discretion.

ABOVE The tucked-in canopy bed of the Sir Percy Blakeney suite OPPOSITE, CLOCKWISE FROM TOP LEFT The Regency style in the dining room of the Sir Percy Blakeney suite; the elegant ceiling and chandelier of the Jane Austen suite; the oak barrel dipping tubs at the property's beloved spa

STON EASTON PARK NEAR BATH, SOMERSET

$\mathcal{S}$ET IN RURAL Somerset, near the Mendip Hills, just fifteen minutes from Bath, the Grade I–listed Ston Easton Park realizes the classic fantasy of staying in a towering, eighteenth-century grand manor house (think *Gosford Park)*, with such characteristic English trimmings as a soaring stone façade, tremendous manicured gardens, and neighboring grazing cows. Built to impress, the Palladian-style mansion sits on thirty-six acres of parkland along the River Norr, perfect for gala events with its long front lawn, imposing seven-foot door, and wide gravel parking lot that seems to anticipate the arrival of a Rolls-Royce. Winding along the driveway through the glistening grass (the weather in the West Country is often wet) and classical park landscape created by renowned eighteenth-century landscape gardener Humphry Repton feels bizarrely familiar—as if the scene was stolen right out of your subconscious.

The former private home of the Hippisley family, whose crest remains carved into the ornate ceiling of the salon, the house was saved from demolition in 1950 due the discovery of an eighteenth-century plunge pool, then bought in 1960 by a former editor of the *Times*, William Rees-Mogg, who spent years restoring it. Today, the house is part of the private hotel conglomerate Von Essen Group, which has helped refurbish the guest rooms and update the rose and kitchen garden.

Perhaps more than any other manor house I visited, the twenty-two-room Ston Easton is most evocative of a time gone by.

From her symmetrical, tall Georgian windows to the historic gardens with such contemporaneous features as an eighteenth-century ice house, romantic Palladian bridges crossing the neighboring River Norr, and a ruined grotto fountain, the house and its antique-filled interiors offer the closest thing to time travel. Not only is the house authentically rich in detail, it is wonderfully grand in architecture and décor, with an opulent state room featuring damask wallpaper, brocade curtains, embroidered upholstery, and towering flower arrangements. Quintessential rooms like the library or the print room—one of England's earliest surviving examples—maintain the traditional layout of the house, while the original kitchen, located below the ground floor, offers an intimate glimpse at a well-preserved Edwardian-era kitchen, complete with copper pans and aged ovens. Ston Easton's modern kitchen, however, is anything but antiquated, and the fine-dining Sorrel Restaurant churns out mouthwatering dishes with ingredients sourced right from the impressive Victorian kitchen garden. My simple vegetable accompaniment—vegetables steamed and boiled in their own jus—was so incredibly delicious that I was taken aback by its basic preparation. Chef Matthew Butcher, previously of Le Manoir aux Quat'Saisons, is a first-time head chef, earning his stripes at the Sorrel Restaurant and seemingly finding no problem commanding a full kitchen and delivering high-quality fare worthy of his former employer. As pleasurable as the meal, the dining

room's white oak-paneled walls and smooth, gray and beige fabrics with slight aqua trim and weave on the chairs and inside the curtains deliver similar levels of sophistication, as does Jasper Conran's Chinoiserie Green pattern for Wedgwood china. Of course, the bucolic view over the backyard and the flowing River Norr ensures a romantic ambiance.

Beyond walking the stunning, historic garden grounds (garden tours from the head gardener are well worth the request), the area provides plenty of activities, including horseback rides along the river and a challenging round of golf at the neighboring Farrington Golf Club. A visit to Ston Easton Park hardly requires second thought if historic manor houses set in the luscious English parkland tickle your fancy. What's special about Ston Easton is that it is charming year-round, from roaring fires in winter to light summer evenings and a seasonal menu bound to impress.

ROOMS

The twenty-two rooms at Ston Easton are decorated individually with color schemes and antique furnishings that appear intended to transport guests back in time as well as comfort them. With grand dimensions, period furniture, and oil-based artwork depicting the Georgian heydey, the rooms first envelop the guest in classic style and then delight them with modern surprises like renovated bathrooms and reliable Internet service. Divided into four

PAGE 48 The imposing façade at Ston Easton Park OPPOSITE The magnificent rose gardens behind Ston Easton
BELOW Beautiful embroidered upholstery in the Chinese Room

categories—classic, superior, deluxe, and
state—the rooms are generously spread
around the enormous house, divided among
three floors, and tucked down enough narrow hallways to make the first venture back a
bit of a challenge. The four state rooms are
clearly the top choice, with their original
Chippendale four-poster beds, generous layout, and sumptuous fabrics. I was lucky
enough to stay in Cascade, a decadently
comfortable room with plush bedding, a soft
pastel palette, and large Georgian windows
overlooking the antique gardens and rushing
River Norr. However, my favorite room in
the house is the exquisite Chinese room,
located on the third floor and adorned with
colorful Chinese silk fabrics, a king-sized
bed, and expansive, south-facing views over
the croquet lawn. The sharp oriental blues,
detailed embroidery, and delicate wallpaper
make for a sensual departure into Asia,
smack in the middle of the English countryside. A true departure indeed! Overseen by
interior designer Lindsay Chambers from
TFT Interiors along with company creative
director Andrew Onraet, the consistently
presented, refined décor is among the
house's prized achievements. From the wallpapered drawing room to the oft-requested
Master Bedroom with its original Chippendale four-poster bed and views of the valley
below, Ston Easton maintains a steadfast
elegance throughout every room.

ABOVE Riding boots all in a row; Jasper Conran's modern china adds flair to the traditional dining room

OPPOSITE, CLOCKWISE FROM TOP LEFT Plush bedding in one of the canopy rooms; statuette in the Chinese Room; velvet headboards keep the rooms cozy and lush; the antique-filled parlour room

THE RECTORY HOTEL   MALMESBURY, WILTSHIRE

$\mathcal{L}$IKE YOUR OWN delightfully refurbished ruin in the countryside, the Rectory Hotel feels more like a chic country house updated by style-savvy friends than a restored religious dwelling-cum-hotel. Due to the warm nature of co-owners Jonathan Barry and Julian Muggridge, who are incidentally both stylish and interior-design savvy, the Rectory is inviting and feels wonderfully familiar upon entry. After a visit to Villa Fontelunga in Tuscany (a featured Italian Hideaway), Barry and Muggridge were inspired to do something similar in their native England and promptly began the hunt for a secluded spot in the country. Their intent was to create a charming English hamlet whose disparity between conventional, historic exteriors and fashionable, contemporary design would inspire others just as Fontelunga did them.

A year later, in 2005, they came upon the three-acre Rectory Hotel located just off the main road in the unfortunately named village of Crudwell, on the border of the Cotswolds near the quintessential English stone village of Malmesbury. The original eighteenth-century rectory of the neighboring Episcopal church has been a privately held hotel since 1984. Constructed piecemeal, the building features symmetrical Georgian-style windows on its older backside, while the tangential wings and Cotswold stone garden are more Victorian in design. Barry and Muggridge leaped at first sight of the tired establishment, drawn to the property's elegant bones, including the thirteenth-century dovecote and original stone-cased baptismal pool (now adorned with lily pads).

The juxtaposition of the old with the new is evident right from the gravel entrance, which leads guests through boxwood hedges up to the smooth, refurbished façade, passing contemporary outdoor sculpture, including Charlie Winnick's curious (and massive) *Rolling Summer Cottage* sphere. Yet it's stepping inside the hotel, with its well-chosen furnishings and purposeful details, that demonstrates the success of the Rectory's high-concept décor. A passionate collector, Barry will eagerly share the details of its interior transformation, starting with the complete stripping of the walls to remove dark paint and replace it with a pale tone that highlights the building's original crown moldings and custom doorframes. Each element has a back story of concentrated toil, from sourcing signature pieces, like Jonathan Huxley's gorgeous blue-toned mural *La Cruz* and two patchwork chairs from emerging London design firm Squint, to restoring the original Cotswold stone floors and crafting a Victorian clothes hanger into a magazine rack. The morning room, as Barry calls it, is the first room the guest enters and is thus responsible for the all-important first impression. Fortunately, it captures the eye ferociously with its whimsical fabrics (the patchwork chairs, in particular), curious materials (1950s-era laser-cut metal cubes and reclaimed wood stumps as end tables), and fanciful pieces, like a model wooden sailboat in the window and exotic lamps fashioned from antique French wallpaper rollers. Continuing down the hall, it becomes clear that the Rectory was originally designed as a family home with a center hallway, two drawing rooms, a back kitchen, and a main staircase. A few tight corners and alcoves keep the history of the place alive, while newer additions like an all-glass conservatory and an expanded, wood-paneled dining room (with gorgeous flower arrangements housed in a large porcelain teapot planter) confirm its boutique hotel status.

Perhaps the most exciting room in the house is the library. With its custom red leather bar in the corner and subtle shimmering wallpaper from Osborne & Little, the room entices those prone to appreciate the art of contrast. The two armchairs, one with a bright fuchsia butterfly print by Kenzo, feature patchwork throw pillows of London scenes from Snowden Flood, while a massive photograph of a rock island by David Parker hangs on the opposite wall. There are easily enough conversation pieces in the room to sustain drinks with fellow guests.

A popular site for weddings, the property's back lawns feature sweeping English gardens designed by Mark Lamy of Chelsea Flower Show fame. The relaxed, natural style of the Victorian gardens is accentuated by the seamless addition of France's elegant Firmwell brand iron furniture around the lily pond, though in fitting Rectory fashion, a few of Firmwell's more innovative, updated pieces (the same green chairs that front the Louvre in Paris) are tucked in twos along the perimeter of the upper lawn.

Self-declared foodies, Barry and Muggridge are passionate about the slow-food movement and have developed a

PAGE 54 The Rectory's amusing mixture of modern art against the historic backdrop LEFT The quirky modern details of the hotel's interior; a teacup vase full of fresh buds from the garden OPPOSITE The former baptismal pond at the Rectory Hotel

community vegetable patch alongside their already flourishing personal one, which stocks both the hotel's more formal restaurant and its neighboring, award-winning gastro pub, the Potting Shed. Just across the street, the whitewashed eighteenth-century pub caters to a friendly local crowd, offering such favorites as fish and chips (the chips are triple fried) and a fantastic Ploughman's lunch, which has been dubbed the Rolls-Royce of Ploughman's. I would sincerely consider traveling to England just for another Ploughman's at the Potting Shed. Popular on Friday and Saturday evening with weekenders and locals alike, the pub is in fact at its best on Sunday nights for its heavily attended rendition of the British pub staple: Quiz Night.

Given the owners' combined passion for food and design and their genteel manner, a few nights at the Rectory will leave you feeling not only satiated but also inspired. And perhaps, like them, you'll think about creating your own future hideaway.

ROOMS

The Rectory's previous hoteliers crammed fifteen rooms into the three-story house, while Barry and Muggridge have wisely reduced it to twelve, preferring to value space and comfort over profit. My favorite room, the Leckhampton suite, faces the back, in the Georgian part of the house, with towering windows overlooking the gardens and stone baptismal pond. The room is a top choice for the hotel's many bridal couples due to its spacious bathroom with roll-top tub, king-sized wooden bed, and cream-colored walls with

appeasing Manuel Canovas fabric drapes and accent pillows. The Pennsylvania Room more obviously mixes the traditional with the contemporary, featuring muted green wall color, Queen Anne–upholstered chairs, low beds with kitschy throw pillows by Alfhild Fagel, and vintage-style Roberts transistor radios. Each room is stocked with books—always a good sign—including the darling *English Journeys* collection from Penguin classics. Upstairs are four more rooms with slanted ceilings and soaring views over the small village of eight hundred and surrounding farmland. One room, Crickley, is noted for the fact that the owners kept the original wallpaper: a pink and green floral pattern that mixes well with the antique white desk, Provençal fabric chair, and cream linen headboard. All of the rooms feature Egyptian-cotton sheets (which really do make a difference), plump pillows, and wonderful Arran bath products, which went straight into my luggage after my trial bubble bath.

Staying at the Rectory provides a wonderful, lavish escape from everyday life. The bright interiors and historic grounds—not to mention the swimming pool—make for an uplifting experience overall. Of course, the gracious hosts, Jonathan and Julian, enhance the place with their charm and kind demeanors, while both the restaurant and the pub offer just the right amount of conviviality alongside top fare. At the risk of sounding obvious, I highly recommend the Rectory for a short getaway to England's picturesque countryside. The boutique property not only has all the requisites delivered in high quality but it also has the benefit of being visually rewarding.

ABOVE Deep set, patchwork chairs and an old-fashioned wallpaper roller made into a lamp.
OPPOSITE, CLOCKWISE FROM TOP LEFT A white wicker bed paired with canovas fabric adds
a cheery feel to the most-requested suite; botanical prints and fresh roses in the upstairs
hallway; bright red furnishings make the lounge pop; a guest room's dainty sitting area

Folded into the bottom of the Cotswolds' absurdly picturesque pastureland, Lower Slaughter Manor offers a delightful resting spot from which to explore one of the most attractive (and popular) areas in England. The property takes its less-than-charming name from the resident town, which is actually an old English translation of "muddy place" and sits right below Upper Slaughter Manor. The mud is attributed to the river Eye, which runs through the small village under two idyllic stone footbridges, leaving luscious green banks that beckon from right outside the manor's front gates. The lovely, small village claims only a few sandstone houses, an ancient church with a soaring steeple (and helpful landmark), and neighboring farmland. The setting is so idyllic that the chirping birds and trimmed hedgerows seem staged for guests' benefit. Pulling into the gravel driveway of the manor house feels equally cinematic, with iron tables hosting afternoon tea on silver trays on the front lawn. I was half-expecting Emma Thompson, dressed in a Jane Austen–film costume, to emerge from the hedged gardens.

The house's history dates back to 1443, when it was a convent housing nuns from the order Syon. The property's adjacent dovecote is one of few two-story structures still standing intact and is believed to have provided nourishment for the nuns during wartime. In 1603 the manor was returned to the crown and subsequently granted in 1611 to Sir George Whitmore, whose family held the estate until 1964. In 1655 the noted stonemason Valentine Strong was commissioned to build a house on the property. Although altered over the years, the house retains some of its original interior fittings, including the stone fireplace in the lounge, which bears the date 1658, as well as the elegant paneled ceiling in the drawing room. Alongside the main house is an attractive stable block dating back to 1770, with a central clock tower and an ivy-covered façade. The self-appointed Queen of the Cotswolds, Lower Slaughter Manor graciously sets the bar for quintessential seventeenth-century English manor estates.

This Relais & Châteaux member property impresses upon first sight, with an imposing stone gate, a manicured gravel driveway, and a brilliant purple outline of lavender bushes around the front lawn. The elevated, topiary-accented entrance hints at a grand arrival; however, the first interior sight is a bookshelf full of brochures. Fortunately, the entryway is small and opens into a pleasant front lounge with a gleaming mahogany staircase at the back. Refurbished in 2006 with décor by Robert van Hawk of London's Felbrick Design, the house presents classic English-toned interiors with traditional patterned upholstery, thick full-length curtains, hand-printed Farrow & Ball wallpaper, and a neutral, floral wall-to-wall carpet. The furnishings range from modern high-backed upholstered couches in the sitting room to antique English armchairs in the sitting room, to the showpiece: a Hurst grandfather clock in the main hall.

Catering to day-trippers who come from near and far for the afternoon cream tea (the cinnamon scones with jam and clotted cream are indeed worthy of a detour), a red-vested waiter stands post at the front door. Served either in the handsome gray-walled sitting room, in the bright beige and cream drawing room, or, weather permitting, at one of the umbrella tables on the front lawn, the tea is a must.

The hotel's central yet quiet location in the often overrun Cotswolds (beware of high-season tour buses) makes it an ideal spot to return to after visiting the busier, tourist-attracting towns of Bourton-on-the-Water or Stow-on-the-Wold. The property's sole tennis court and its surrounding country lanes offer options for exercise—particularly desirous after a few meals in the lauded contemporary-style restaurant, sixteen58, awarded three AA Rosettes. Don't miss chef David Kelman's succulent filet of Old Spot pork rolled in Asian spices, the quail egg starter with pancetta and plum puree, or the white chocolate ginger parfait paired with a special dessert wine. With cocoa-colored silk walls, Murano crystal, blue chandeliers, and gold-sheen tablecloths, the restaurant could easily be set in a more modern environment, making the idea that it is instead tucked into a country manor in the Cotswolds, available to only a few guests at a time, undeniably more romantic.

The mullioned windows
of the front entrance

ROOMS

The nineteen rooms at Lower Slaughter
Manor are divided between the main house
and the newer, tangential Coach House
building. All of the rooms offer an unexpected, updated style with luscious pillow-
top mattresses, fresh carpeting, contemporary glass lamps, and a refurbished and clean
feel overall. Every room is stocked with fresh
fruit, water, and a crystal carafe of sherry,
should you feel so inclined.

The top rooms in the Coach House are
the two spacious garden suites: Valentine
and Magnolia, with decadent, custom four-
poster beds and hot tubs on the private patio
gardens. Valentine, the more attractive
(albeit zanier) of the two, is characterized by
its mounds of silk-covered pillows in vibrant
shades of orange, lime green, and purple,
which add welcome splashes of color to the
otherwise muted, masculine palette. The
bed is made of up four twelve-foot white
posters with black spheres on top and a
thick, checkered canopy draped along the
back and sides. The room's appeal is reminiscent of designer Anouska Hempel but
retains some sense of tradition with original
details like a wood-beamed ceiling, a stone
fireplace, and three sets of iron-mullioned
windows. It feels very light despite the slate-
colored drapery and black-lacquered furnishings, while the bathroom is a wonderful,
spoiled affair with twin roll-top tubs staring
out a set of French doors to the private garden. The patio is ideal for in-room dining
and offers a carefree transition from meal to
bed to hot tub and back again. Clearly ideal
for honeymooners or a romantic break, the
Valentine suite is an opulent take on English
contemporary style.

My preferred room in the Coach
House, however, is the Longborough junior
suite, located directly above the Valentine
suite. Its generous, open layout, pillow-top
king-sized bed, and separate dressing room
with feminine accents, including a soft, gray
flannel chaise longue and circular iron-
framed window, give the room a luxurious,
spacious feel, while light cream and taupe
tones on the upholstery, walls, and bedding
keep it fresh and airy. (Don't be put off by
the picture on the Web site.)

In the main house, the eleven rooms
retain their seventeenth-century layout and
dimensions, though with contemporary
décor similar to what exists in the Coach
House. Named after the daughters of the
manor's original family, the Whitmores,
each of the rooms bears its own signature
color scheme and style. My first pick would
be Antoinette, which, as suspected from its
name, presents a French aesthetic complete
with cream-colored Dupioni silk bed curtains, classic French mirrored side tables,
and chocolate brown bullion-fringe table
skirts. The handcrafted four-poster bed is
majestic, five feet off the ground, custom-
made, and equipped with a bedside two-step
ladder, while the bathroom features handsome lizard-print wallpaper and a slipper
bath complete with a view over the front
lawn to the small town of Lower Slaughter.
The commanding view—best taken in from
the wide, oak-framed windows in the bedroom—makes guests feel as if they are in the
most prominent room in the house.

Most rooms at Lower Slaughter Manor
are richly appointed with updated, fresh
bathrooms, fine-quality linen, and charming
historic details (particularly in the main
house). Other favorite rooms include Nina,
with its soothing lilac and beige color combination, and Faye, with its striped window
seat overlooking the tranquil back garden.
With a guaranteed delicious meal and
afternoon tea service, not to mention its
postcard-perfect setting, Lower Slaughter
Manor is ideal for a weekend jaunt to the
Cotswolds and appeals to couples looking to
simply relax and enjoy leisure time together.

OPPOSITE, CLOCKWISE FROM TOP LEFT The main house's cushioned staircase landing; the elegant drawing room; the canopy suite in the main house; twin tubs in the Coach House's Valentine suite ABOVE The contemporarily refurbished parlor

BARNSLEY HOUSE   BARNSLEY, CIRENCESTER

*T*HE BARNSLEY HOUSE, an idyllic seventeenth-century, Grade II–listed manor house in England's beloved Cotswolds area, has long been known to the public for its eleven acres of magnificent English gardens, cultivated by former owners and legendary gardeners David and Rosemary Verey. In 2009, the eighteen-room Cotswold-stone mansion was acquired by the owners of nearby Calcot Manor and refurbished with a smooth, contemporary décor, a new holistic spa, and a delicious restaurant and gastropub. As a result, Barnsley House is now attracting non-horticulturists alongside garden devotees and making the property one of the Cotswolds' top stays.

Fortunately the new owners of Barnsley House were sensitive during the renovations and deferred to the historic character of the beautiful stone mansion by instilling interiors with simple, muted colors and modern and unobtrusive furnishings from the likes of B&B Italia. Despite the striking contrast of a modern design style with traditional architecture, the overall unfussy nature of the interior décor instead enhances the building's original stone fireplaces, exposed beams, and wood floors. The lounge area, a successful take on mod-cozy, instantly communicates a lived-in comfort that appears to have welcomed many despite being fairly new.

Given that the hotel is located in a popular tourist destination, area attractions are bountiful, from fly-fishing to cycling to hot-air ballooning—that is, if you can tear yourself away from the property, particularly the Garden Spa overlooking the meadow. Designed by Stephen Woodhams with the intent of bringing the gardens indoors, the contemporary-design spa features floor-to-ceiling windows, drystone walls, and five treatment rooms with aromatic herbs hanging from the exposed beams. From the hydrotherapy pool (and the cozy lounge chairs surrounding it) to the heavy focus on herbal and floral scents in the treatments, the revamped spa turns a weekend at Barnsley into a complete package of indulgence.

The dining options at Barnsley House are further impetus to stay put. The formal Potager Restaurant overlooks the lush gardens, and produce from the vegetable garden enhances chef Graham Grafton's Italian-influenced English cuisine. Neither too fussy nor oversimplified, the menu at Potager is ideally satisfying though small, while the setting overlooking the gardens—especially the tables by the bay window—keeps the experience feeling fresh. Gather your group or loved one for a private dinner in the garden Temple and you're guaranteed a memorable evening. (This is a hint to the all the guys looking for a beautiful place to propose!)

Despite the allure of Barnsley House's homegrown fare or the thirty-seat cinema, it's the resplendent gardens that make the country house a true standout among Cotswolds-area properties (not to mention a fabulous backdrop for a private celebration). With botanical features and adornments like statues by Simon Verity, an ornamental fruit and vegetable garden, and a laburnum walk, the gardens at Barnsley House are the property's crown jewel, drawing a paying public during the day. Designed in the late 1950s by Rosemary Verey and embellished with architectural structures like the Temple from Fairford Park by her husband, David, the gardens have been attracting students and visitors since the 1970s, including the Prince of Wales, who visited Rosemary and the gardens regularly until her death in 2001. Tantalizingly attractive with their formal lawns, sun-filled terraces, knot gardens, and secret corners, the grounds at Barnsley House compel guests to stroll, picnic, or just lounge (on the grass since cushioned seats are minimal) among their flowering, dappled sweetness.

For nights or midday meals with less formality, don't miss the local Village Pub, recently refurbished with understated cool tones and evident respect for the building's original wood beams, stone walls, and picture windows. The pub fare is consistently tasty, while the local scene provides ample people-watching opportunities and a welcome respite from neighboring tourist traps. The pub also offers seven guest rooms, though I far recommend booking at Barnsley House instead, if only for the floral views. Most important, staying at the recently revamped Barnsley House makes visiting the Cotswolds attractive again. Its noted departure from various overdone or kitschy neighbors and the investment in its natural surroundings have created the ideal combination of a relaxed, serene setting with a popular (and yes, still worth visiting) destination.

PAGE 66 Known for its gardens, Barnsley House makes quite a fragrant impression OPPOSITE, CLOCKWISE FROM TOP LEFT Clay pitchers set an earthy tone; the casual, muted décor of the sitting room; exposed beams in a guest room lend a country feel; leather and wood play off each other in the bar ABOVE The lush legacy of Rosemary Verey FOLLOWING PAGES A gardener's paradise at Barnsley House

ROOMS

The guest rooms at Barnsley House continue the cool, contemporary décor of the hotel's ground floor and restaurant. Adorned with furnishings from London interior designer Fox Linton, the rooms differ in size and layout, though all feature crisp, comfortable linens under white duvets, plasma flat-screen TVs (some at the foot of the bed), and absolutely no signs of chintz. Décor details like recessed lighting, leather headboards, polished wood floors, and, as expected, fresh flowers give the rooms a pleasant, sanctuary feel—especially those with terraces or balconies. However, it's the bathrooms that deserve the rave reviews, with their roll-top tubs, double vanities, walk-in showers with subway-tiled floors,

and televisions. Room 1 has twin bathtubs, should you prefer to bathe side by side, while Room 2 has a Jacuzzi under a dazzling bulb chandelier.

My favorite room is Room 7, the Rosemary Verey Suite. With its private conservatory dining area, small garden, and terrace, not to mention a sumptuous four-poster bed and double-occupancy roll-top tub, it allows guests to indulge in extra privacy and relish the opportunity to enjoy the garden setting—just as Rosemary would have intended. The recently added six Stableyard rooms and suites (numbers 14 to 19) offer more space with duplex layouts and a richer décor that mixes deep reds and blacks. I'm also partial to the Davina suite (Room 8),

which has a pleasing, open layout with a generous sofa, dining room table (ideal if work must follow you), and the requisite roll-top tub; however, it's the room's beam ceiling and cozy white and wood palette that feel extra welcoming. The Potting Shed, another top suite, is totally removed from the hotel, a true hideaway room with a wood-burning stove, a private garden, and considerably more country-style décor and ambiance. I found it peaceful, though admittedly not as fresh or carefully maintained as the rooms in the main building. Overall, the rooms at Barnsley House hit all the necessary marks—luxuriously appointed, clean, and comfortable—essential elements for a proper hideaway stay.

LE MANOIR AUX QUAT'SAISONS   GREAT MILTON, OXFORD

THE REALIZED FANTASY of two-Michelin-starred superchef Raymond Blanc, Le Manoir aux Quat'Saisons, a Victorian English country-house hotel and fine-dining restaurant, is a testament to the gourmand's notorious perfectionism and eye for superior detail. An unmistakable reference to Blanc's native France, Le Manoir sits nestled in the Oxfordshire countryside, surrounded by bushels of lavender, professional-grade herb and vegetable patches, and a finely manicured rose garden, offering guests the intoxicating (and signature French) combination of exquisite cuisine alongside superb, refined style.

Open since 1984, Le Manoir is hardly off the beaten track. In fact, it is one of England's most sought-after destinations, often reserved by guests for special occasions and once-in-a-lifetime celebrations. While I was there, I witnessed a delighted mother being treated to the daily tasting lunch by her son, who had spent a year saving for it. It is a common occurrence, or so I was told, and one Monsieur Blanc is adamant about honoring, demanding of his staff that every guest be treated like the most important person in the room no matter their length of stay. As a result, the staff at Le Manoir, particularly the dining servers, are notably polished, and the entire affair, from the menu presentation over canapés served in the drawing room to the unforgettable three-tier cheese tray at the close of the meal, is executed with a professional grace and dignity that borders on theater. I must say, even as someone in a profession filled with indulgences, dining at Le Manoir is a rapturous experience, especially if you enjoy being spoiled through your stomach, one morsel at a time.

Lauded for its imaginative cuisine and organic bent, Le Manoir's modern French restaurant relies heavily on the fresh ingredients grown right on site in Blanc's impressive vegetable and herb garden, with ninety types of vegetables and more than seventy different herbs. Given the restaurant's pilgrimage status, it's best to reserve far in advance, and never assume that an overnight booking at the hotel ensures you a table at the restaurant for dinner. Be sure to request a table in the atrium space overlooking the gardens rather than the cramped front room. Both lunch and dinner (and even breakfast, though admittedly a less decadent affair) offer tasting menus with paired wines and a wide array of flavors and culinary triumphs. Though the atrium dining room is light-filled during the day, it is especially alluring at dusk, when the evening glow softens the garden view and the candles just begin to garner relevance. I highly recommend dinner over lunch so you can fully indulge, with only a short trudge back to your room. Due to the richness and elaborateness of the meal, I also suggest you make your reservation time earlier than normal so you can start the culinary journey, which begins with drinks and canapés, no later than 7 P.M. This way, you can truly take your time, savoring every mouthful and noting every detail without the threat of bedtime exhaustion.

If you find yourself so inspired or are already a chef in the making, I recommend studying Blanc's method with his onsite cooking school.

ROOMS

The style of Le Manoir's thirty-two guest rooms was conceived by Raymond and executed by his design partner, Emily Todhunter, with whom he has worked for eighteen years. He credits her superior design knowledge and sensitivity, while she remarks on his perfectionism and profound desire for the guests to have "the most amazing time." Equipped with WiFi and flat-screen televisions, all rooms offer top-quality modern amenities alongside thoughtful, detailed décor (and some of the most luscious bath amenities). Divided between the main house and the tangential conservatory building known as the garden wing, the "superior rooms" and "signature suites" offer guests immense selection and even include a room housed in an original fifteenth-century dovecote. The newest ones, two garden rooms and two suites, are Raymond's most recent triumph. Blanc à Blanc, a totally white room, was inspired by Versailles, with such exquisite details as delicate embroidery on the headboard and a glass chandelier. Jade is an exotic departure inspired by Blanc's travels in southeast Asia, with marble sculptures and a slate-gray bathroom. L'Orangerie is a celebration of French classicism, with stone tables, fruit trees, and soft pastel colors in a large space.

PAGE 73 The lavender-lined pathways surrounding Le Manoir ABOVE The most elaborate cheese-tray in England; The mullioned windows of the Lavender suite OPPOSITE The soothing interiors of the elegant Hollyhock Guestroom

Lace, Blanc's favorite, is a sexy tribute to women, with deep reds, black, and, of course, various applications of lace. These four rooms are featured on the Web site in a video of Raymond explaining their aesthetic formulation and showcasing his genuine passion and personal involvement in the hotel's décor.

Despite the elaborate amenities (private gardens, Bose speaker systems, outdoor courtyards, twin soaking tubs, and separate sitting rooms) and opulence of the suites at Le Manoir—some are so large you could host your own cocktail party—my personal preference are the delicate rooms found in the old main house. Located on the second floor, the Lavande suite is the main house's largest room, featuring a commanding view through a mullioned bay window over the front lawn and the twin rows of lavender.

Cozy furnishings include a plush, purple-hued sofa facing a wood-burning fireplace, warm oak flooring, and a velvet-pillow-strewn bed that's especially forgiving after an indulgent meal downstairs. I was particularly pleased with the silver tray of fresh fruit, two large bottles of sparkling and still water, Waterford crystal glasses, and a carafe of Madeira. A notable downside of the room is its entrance next to the powder rooms utilized by dining guests. During mealtime the traffic can provide a slight noise irritant, though fortunately the bed and bathroom are farthest away from the door.

The Orchid "superior" room is actually the smallest in this category and is very cramped, relative to the ample suites in the garden wing. However, the soothing, contemporary cream-colored décor, multiple orchid plants, and textured grass-paper walls

from Nobilis gave me an instant feeling of fresh, homey comfort, as if one were staying at a friend's house. Given the tight space, especially in the bathroom, the room is best suited for single travelers or those just in for a night.

Hollyhock, which is in the front of the house, overlooks the courtyard and is perhaps the most traditionally appointed room in the house and filled with antiques. Originally the master bedroom of the Cromwell family, Hollyhock features a large bay window framed by heavy cream curtains, hand-painted wallpaper from Ian Harper, and a spacious marble bathroom. Incidentally, both Orchid and Hollyhock are designed by Emily Todhunter, whose airy, light style and preference for traditional, soft palettes seem especially appealing to me when basking in the warm afterglow of a Raymond Blanc meal.

OPPOSITE, CLOCKWISE FROM TOP LEFT A reading corner in Hollyhock; Ian Harper's masterful wallpaper offset by the romantic fabric canopy; silk upholstery in the Orchid Room; the darling Orchid Room's bed ABOVE Zoffany fabric pillows add pizzazz to the tranquil scheme of Hollyhock

VINE HOUSE
BURNHAM MARKET, NORFOLK

*H*IDDEN IN PLAIN sight, the tiny, ivy-covered Vine House boutique hotel sits nestled in a row of town houses facing the center green of the darling seventeenth-century seaside village of Burnham Market on Norfolk's north coast. Referred to by some as "Harry and Will's country," meaning that it's the sort of place the royal family and their posh friends might visit, Burnham Market is unabashedly preppy and charming. Main Street is lined with art galleries, boutiques selling high-priced homemade soaps and Shetland blankets, a musty bookstore, and a bustling pub. Locals chat over pints on the picnic tables of the town pub, the Hoste Arms Hotel, while shopping-bag-laden ladies stroll the street, fielding their children's cries for ice cream from the truck parked on the center green. With its central location and unassuming residential façade, Vine House offers instant (and informal) access to all the quintessential summertime action.

Owned by the Hoste Arms Hotel, located directly across the green, the seven-bedroom Vine House relies on the larger hotel for its daily housekeeping service, cocktail-hour butler service, and occasional made-to-order meals. In stark contrast to the bustling Hoste Arms, Vine House offers exclusivity and guaranteed peace and quiet. Check-in takes place at the Hoste Arms, and as soon as you've been given your key and directed to park in Vine House's reserved alley off Main Street, the sweet tinge of privilege hits you. Opened on Valentine's Day of 2008, Vine House was built with the lofty ambition of creating the "best boutique hotel outside of London" by passionate owners, the late Paul Whittome and his wife Jeanne. Right away, the Georgian brick house with a robin's-egg-blue door and small iron sign entices its guests as a fresh, smart spot.

On the interior, the soft palette of grays and pale blues offset by whitewashed walls with gilded frames and mirrors relaxes your senses and welcomes you with a bright, updated sensibility that perfectly fits the chic town and seaside location. Absent of fussy English curios, Vine House features a welcome, cool décor brightened with subtle details like Victorian-style crystal and brass sconces, colorful ticking on the neutral floor-length curtains, and aqua-toned throw pillows to accent the divan in the living room. The ground floor of the house is hardly spacious, with just two sitting rooms and a small back mudroom with a cupboard for wellies, but fortunately guests are rarely stuck inside. The small front drawing room looks out on the street and features a handsome Knole sofa with bullion fringe and two high-backed velvet armchairs that offer the perfect perch for reading. Further through the house lies the central living room, whose elegant linen curtains frame large windows out to the back patio, with its rose-covered pergola, growing vines (the namesake of the property), and fragrant garden. The décor is wonderfully stylish yet personable, and making oneself comfortable is as difficult as relaxing at a friend's house.

Every night the living room and patio (weather permitting) host a charming evening cocktail hour serviced by a personal Vine House butler. Otherwise meals are taken over at the Hoste Arms, whose dinner service far exceeded expectations (don't miss the oysters). Service is one of Paul Whittome's enduring tenets. On the entryway table at Vine House is a white phone and small sign that says, "Lift the receiver for tea, coffee, or any other form of assistance." Also, breakfast can be delivered in a wicker hamper to your room—a special treat for those visiting with romantic intentions or simply when the winter chill is up. Not surprisingly, Burnham Market is festively adorned and fabulously cozy during Christmas season, making wintertime visits extra tempting.

ROOMS

All seven guest rooms at Vine House present soft, contemporary color schemes (beige, cream, aqua, lilac) with patterned wallpapers from Osborne & Little, high-thread-count linens, and the rare English country amenity of air-conditioning. My top choice is Room 57, with a fresh and floral fragrance in the air, a picture-perfect bowl of fresh strawberries sprinkled with powdered sugar, and one of the most alluring bathrooms I found in England. Tucked up in the alcove of the second floor, facing the back of the house and overlooking the small back garden, the room is cozy, with thoughtful adornments, not unlike a well-designed guest room at that same stylish friend's house. The tufted headboard is both modern and classic with its appealing curved shape, while the metallic damask wallpaper and matching gilt sconces give the room a Venetian flavor. In an

effort to elongate the room's somewhat tight dimensions, a massive, gilt-framed mirror hangs opposite the bed. However, the small-sized room gains immediate favor with its decadent bathroom featuring gray French doors, a claw-foot tub set center stage, separate walk-in shower, and double porcelain vanities. The back wall of the bathroom is decorated

with ornamental tiles, while those in the shower have been hand-painted with a feminine, floral design. A crystal chandelier hangs ceremoniously over the tub, as if the guests needed any further encouragement toward a bubble bath.

Alas, the rooms have some drawbacks, including thin walls, no nightly turndown

service, and no complimentary drinking water. Nevertheless, for a pleasant visit to the Norfolk coast, where activities like sailing lessons, golf, fishing, and even seal watching make it an ideal destination for families and active travelers alike, Vine House provides just the spot for a delightful home away from home.

OPPOSITE, CLOCKWISE FROM TOP LEFT Room 57's corner bed; a warm mixture of blues and creams in the parlor; elegant antiques in the entryway; tassel details on the parlor curtains ABOVE The soothing robin's-egg-blue walls of the entryway; the Knole sofa in the front reading room

PEACOCK AT ROWSLEY MATLOCK, DERBYSHIRE

RIGHT ON THE corner of the A6 as it runs through the small town of Rowsley in Derbyshire's famed Peak District, the Peacock at Rowsley is a favored haunt for fly-fisherman, anglers, and avid walkers drawn to this lush area along the rivers Wye and Derwent. The boutique property of just sixteen rooms caters to a relaxed clientele that appreciates the updated aesthetic (electric-green velvet chairs and whitewashed walls) alongside a traditional stone-walled pub and various antique wood furnishings. Recently acquired by Lord Edward Manners, owner of the nearby Haddon Hall, the Peacock underwent an extensive refurbishment in 2005 with design accents provided by award-winning Parisian designer India Mahdavi.

The atmosphere of the Peacock is demonstrably relaxed. The easy, clean appointment of the drawing room and the old English feel of the pub allow for anglers or walkers to come right in without having to change. The Peacock offers two types of dining: basic fare in the hotel's pub, ideal for weary travelers, and the restaurant for those spending more than two nights. Head chef Dan Smith has worked with Tom Aitkins in London and bestows his big-city talent using local fare. With an impressive wine list shared with the restaurant, the pub enjoys a healthy following among people merely enjoying a drink to those interested in a full meal. Both the restaurant and pub are outfitted in Englishman Robert Mouseman's heralded early twentieth-century wood furniture, with its signature church-mouse relief embedded into the designs. The pub's steak frites comes with onion rings and crisps (french fries), making it the obvious choice for those feeling at their fittest. It washes down nicely with the local Peak Ale beer on tap. The fourteen-seat private dining room is another pleasant space, with deep purple walls, an antique dining table, and windows looking out over the garden. Though located on a well-trafficked corner, the hotel has a substantial hedged-in garden with tables and umbrellas for alfresco dining.

The Peacock is clearly aimed at fishermen, offering seven miles of world-renowned fly-fishing with rare wild rainbow trout and a unique strain of brown trout. Each morning a gillie from Haddon Hall can be seen pacing downstairs, waiting to escort guests to the river Wye, while the receptionist is busy organizing directions to various walks for other guests. For non-fishermen, the hotel is ideally located for visiting nearby Haddon Hall and historic Chatsworth House. Given the active nature of the hotel, most of the guests can be seen in some semblance of Gore-Tex clothing at breakfast, a healthy spread that will provide energy for the day. Additionally, the hotel leaves a cheerful daily newsletter on the table at breakfast, which is as useful (offering the day's weather or a recommended daily walk) as it is charming (with a quote of the day and a bit of local history).

Dressed herself in outdoorsy, comfortable apparel typical of the Midlands, general manager Jenni MacKenzie bustles about, ready to do what needs to be done. Typical of a crowd on an active holiday, the mood of the hotel is spirited and unpresumptuous. All in all, the Peacock at Rowsley is a comfortable haven for visitors compelled to tour the scenic area and its natural spoils.

ROOMS

The bedrooms fan out on the second floor of the house and feature simple antique furniture and various fine fabrics sourced from London, Paris, New York, and Milan. There are two rooms on the third floor but they are small and cramped, so it's best to avoid them. Number 5, one of the "special rooms" and also known as the Four-Poster Room, is one of the largest and certainly most comfortable in the house. The other "special room" is noted for its antique bed originally from Belvoir Castle, though the layout is not as spacious as the Four-Poster. Located at the front of the house, the Four-Poster Room overlooks the busy corner road through three lovely mullioned windows. The windows are double-paned in an attempt to alleviate traffic noise and presumably this does help somewhat, but cars and trucks are still notable during the day. Fortunately, drawing the attractive French blue floor-length curtains keeps the morning and evening light at bay (this is particularly useful in summer, when it doesn't get dark until 11 P.M.). The traditional-style room adds a bit of pop with a brightly painted aqua back wall, setting a striking contrast against the black cast-iron fireplace, antique chestnut armoire, and carved chest. The marble bathroom is newly refurbished with a great shower (necessary

PAGE 84 The comforting stone and wood palette of the hotel's pub
OPPOSITE The hard-to-miss signage of Peacock at Rowsley BELOW Antique fixtures nestled in the ivy

after a day spent warring nature's elements) and heated floors, though a bit awkwardly located behind the bed. The rest of the larger double rooms face the back garden and offer a quieter night's sleep in king-sized beds with flat-screen TVs and DVD players for snug movie nights in bed. (The Peacock has quite an impressive DVD library for guests.) Other top room choices are Room 11, for its zanier décor with a poppy-patterned wallpaper alongside beautiful cross-hatched mullioned windows, Room 9 for its aubergine-painted back wall and high ceilings, and of course, Room 3 for the beautiful upholstered sleigh bed and its light-filled corner setting. For a wonderfully cozy stop in the Midlands, or better yet, a weekend of serious fishing, the rooms at Peacock at Rowsley meet all the necessary requirements for a comfortable and pleasant stay.

ABOVE Room 5's bright aqua wall and plush four-poster bed OPPOSITE, CLOCKWISE FROM TOP LEFT An original window handle; the pub's local brew and original church-pew seating; plum walls; Room 8's mellow burgundy back wall; Room 5's crosshatch mullioned windows

THE GEORGE IN RYE RYE, EAST SUSSEX

Situated on one of Rye's main veins, the popular-with-the-locals George in Rye hotel occupies a Listed building with all its original bones, tight corners, and narrow hallways lovingly exposed. "The George," as it's known, is Rye's oldest coaching inn, originally established in 1575, and given that it predates King George, its name is rumored to have come from St. George. Originally closer to the water, the inn was relocated to High Street in 1719, though its white, eighteenth-century façade acts as a frontispiece for a timber structure at least two hundred years older. The inn also expanded over the years, pushing into its neighboring buildings, while a central courtyard was created behind the street. In fact, the building alone can speak to the development changes of the town over the years.

The George carries an illustrious past, having entertained three King Georges, Wellington, and the mayor of London, and later became the town's posting and meeting house, hosting notable banquets (including one honoring Napoleon's defeat). Sadly, in the mid-twentieth century the George fell into a sincere state of neglect, pottering on solely on name. Then in 2004, the current owners, transplanted Londoners Katie Clarke and her husband, Alex, bought the George and lovingly returned it to its rightful, center-court stature.

After a two-year-long refurbishment, including the restoration of the building's multiple original details and historical elements, the twenty-four-room hotel reopened in 2006, showcasing an updated, contemporary décor. Utilizing the perfectionist and detail-oriented skills from her career in set design, Katie, along with her designer friend Maria Speake, oversaw the entire process, personally redecorating and refining each room of the house. As a result, the George is sophisticated with just the right historical measure and wonderfully atmospheric.

The upstairs of the George is one big, winding hallway with various small staircases and wood-framed doorways—the result of combining tangential houses. The tight space and awkward turns are made cheerful with rainbow-striped sisal carpeting and hand-painted directions on the walls. The original ballroom is still intact and used frequently for weddings, accommodating up to 120 people. The Victorian floral wallpaper panels by de Gournay and crystal chandeliers offer an elegant atmosphere for receptions, while the adjoining meeting room with its corner bar is perfect for hosting cocktails.

The George's intimate thirty-seat restaurant is just off the reception area and serves breakfast, lunch, and dinner daily. Head chef Rod Grossmann smiles broadly when asked about his local producers, touting the famous nearby salt marshes, where the Marleys Roywle lamb, known as "the best lamb in England," breeds. Indeed, the lamb dinner entrée is one of the best I have ever tasted, and with a simple accompaniment of cumin-cooked carrots and eggplant, it struck the appropriate chord of homemade goodness in the cozy dining room setting.

The pièce de résistance of the George, and clearly the locals agree, is the traditional-style pub, the George Tap. The Tap's refurbishment was a focal point of the Clarkes, who salvaged everything they could, using detailed measures like sandblasting the Elizabethan wood beams back to their original color, ensuring that the stone fireplace works again, and mounting the 250-year-old Gill Parliamentary wood clock in the entryway. The pub's evident popularity can also be credited to its comfortable furnishings: a cracked leather sectional decorated with pale blue throw pillows, sets of upholstered gentleman chairs, and generous leather square-top stools. On pleasant days, the back garden courtyard, accessible either through the pub or the tunnel entrance off the street, offers an attractive alfresco option. With its Freeline teak tables and cushioned chairs, dark gray umbrellas, and potted, square-shaped centerpieces, the courtyard offers one of the best mixtures of a relaxed yet well-appointed setting for a home-cooked pub meal or pint in the south of England. Meanwhile, the view of the varied backs of buildings, with their tapestry of materials—stone, brick shingle, dark weather-stained wood actually furthers the decorative ambiance, as does the landscaping of towering bamboo shoots, eucalyptus trees, and ficus plants. Of course, the ten taps, including the locally brewed Harveys Ale, and the beloved pork scratchings (don't ask, just try) also do their part to keep you satiated.

The surrounding area has plenty for guests to explore. Offering everything from bird-watching in the harbor to windsurfing lessons at the beach to perusing the antique

PAGE 90 The vintage-inspired décor in Room 8 ABOVE The remodeled pub, the George Tap;
The George's cappuccino OPPOSITE The cozy back deck provides alfresco dining at the George

and glass experts' shops down the road from the hotel, Rye is a quaint spot to spend a weekend, and the George makes it worth the journey.

ROOMS

All twenty-four guest rooms at the George have been individually designed according to their quirky layouts, slanting walls, and varying dimensions. Katie passionately sought to highlight each room's assets while maintaining her adage of giving people what they want out of a hotel stay: a big, comfy bed, fresh linen that is better than what they have at home, and intriguing style. Room 1, the largest, is located right off the side-street entrance to the pub's garden courtyard. Two large bay windows provide ample light, which bounces off the silver-accented fur-

nishings and chrome lamps. The room's navy blue and teal palette mixes soothingly with the gray-striped walls, beige wool sisal carpeting, and four-poster bed with corduroy-upholstered frame. The bathroom is deliciously large, with both a claw-foot roll-top tub and a large walk-in rain shower.

Room 14 on the rooftop is accessed through an Alice in Wonderland–sized door followed by a tight staircase, and therefore feels very private. The sizable bathroom features a shuttered window and marble roll-top tub angled at a diagonal in the center or the room and is stocked with REN products. All of the rooms have large, flat-screen televisions on the walls, Tivoli radios, and Vi-Spring beds with Frette linens.

Room 8 is my clear favorite. With its appealing cocoa and orange palette, velvet-embroidered linen curtains, handsome

faded orange linen antique desk chair, and massive rosewood armoire, it has just the right mix of old and new. Continuing the theme is the bed's modern, chocolate-colored suede headboard and cream vintage-stitched quilt. The room's best feature is its unique location in the very back of the hotel, with windows overlooking both the side street and the garden courtyard. The bathroom is a bit cramped and the tub is tucked into an alcove in the room, but the amount of light, the large corduroy sectional couch with Neisha Crossland fabric pillows, and the funky sloping ceiling make it all the more charming. Spending the morning among the goose-down pillows and duvet and ordering cappuccinos to the room while listening to Rye's persistent seagull symphony is highly recommended.

ABOVE Room 1's deep blues offer instant relaxation; the corner vanity in Room 1 OPPOSITE, CLOCKWISE FROM TOP LEFT The 250-year-old Gill Parliamentary clock; worn, leather corner couches in the pub; the traditional drawing room with roaring fire; another English George (George Harrison)

SWAN HOUSE HASTINGS

STEPS AWAY FROM the antique-lovers' High Street in the Old Town area of Hastings (the quaint, pretty part), sits the charming, four-bedroom Swan House. Dating back to 1490, the Grade II–listed house retains such authentic historic details as original beam ceilings, oak floors, and distinctive fifteenth-century second-story sliding-glass windows. Rather unassuming from the exterior, the black-and-white-painted façade, slanted walls, and simple oak door communicate the building's age, while the hanging geranium pots and swirly script lettering in the window are the sole indications that the place is expecting visitors. Opened in May 2006 by Irishman Brendan McDonagh and his business partner, fashion designer Lionel Copley, Swan House feels surprisingly spacious despite its antiquated dimensions and small offering of four guest rooms. This is due entirely to the gentle hospitality of Brendan and the unfussy, pale-colored décor against the antique surroundings, which set the appealing tranquil mood of Swan House.

The main sitting room features a cozy seating area with two plush couches strewn with navy and white pillows and a coffee table, made from salvaged wood found on Hastings beach, facing the seventeenth-century fireplace. The mood is wonderfully relaxed and the space is attractively appointed, with low, exposed-beam ceilings, iron-grate windows—one with stained glass from Poland—and various showpieces like the hand-blown glass bauble floor light from Morocco and the horn mirror constructed of resin. Daisy, the friendly Jack Russell, will gladly snuggle up next to you. With a true passion for Swan House and the treasures of Hastings Old Town, Brendan will happily share the origins of each antique furnishing, considering that they were all sourced locally. For instance, the subtle, three-dimensional woven wool wallpaper in the entryway is a particular highlight, found at High Street Retro Centre, a shop just up the street.

Although there is no restaurant at Swan House, breakfast is served each morning with beautiful presentation and locally sourced ingredients, all prepared by Brendan himself. The marble table in the luscious back garden or the oak table in the main room is colorfully set with designer placemats and napkins from John Lewis, plus a printed single-sheet menu. As one would hope, the coffee is rich and strong, the orange juice is freshly squeezed, and Brendan's daily smoothie makes a healthy and delicious starter. If you're up for it, I recommend the Swan's full English breakfast, which includes homemade beans.

Brendan is the consummate host, sensitive to his guests and never pushy or too chatty. Nevertheless, be sure to ask his advice on the day's activities or meals out. He is a wonderful source of information and will gladly recommend his favorite local haunts, from shops to pubs to restaurants with sea views. Given his refined sensibilities, his suggestions make him a worthy ambassador for the location. Hastings is a premier antiquing and vintage junk destination. Although many visit Hastings for the beach, its seaside attractions (theme parks make it a great family destination), and famous fish and chips, for me, Hastings Old Town, with its charming shops and winding streets, is the true gem and certainly the place to stay.

ROOMS

The four guest rooms at Swan House are accessed by two separate entrances, making it ideal for couples traveling together or a family taking over two rooms comfortably. The rooms accessed from the first floor include a small single room with an arched set of oak doors opening onto the fragrant back garden and a second-floor room, with a private staircase and inviting French antique bed. The other two rooms are located up the ancient, slanted staircase, made less treacherous by an attractive Turkish goat-hair runner. Filled with natural light, the two front rooms feature whimsical décor, like hand-painted wall designs and fluffy white duvets and Provençal blankets on the beds. The first room on the left, Maison, is my first choice, with its spacious, square layout, private balcony overlooking the garden, and antique striped armoire that's reminiscent of French beach cabanas. The room's immediate appeal is due to the fresh gray and white palette. From the white linen curtains to the European quilted gray pillows to the Victorian garden chair and stuffed white couch, the furnishings and simple design keep the room feeling breezy and clean. The house's considerable age is evident through the creaky floorboards and low, slanted ceilings,

PAGE 96 The Swan House's historic, Grade-I listed façade ABOVE The cool, crisp interiors of the guest rooms OPPOSITE The darling back garden table set for breakfast

but Brendan has chosen to highlight the antiquity by creating contrast with bright rooms, vintage fixtures in the bathrooms (which I'm thankful are not antiquated), and soft, French country–inspired interior design. Worth noting, the proximity to the sea means seagulls are nearby, providing a constant caw that may seem jarring at first

light; however, the gusts of sea air will lull you right back to sleep. Restricted from major construction due to the building's age and historical importance, Swan House has triumphed by offering impeccable service and fresh, clean, and comfortable guest rooms, providing a desired break from your everyday existence.

AUTHOR'S NOTE Brendan is currently at work refurbishing another property in Hastings, the Old Rectory, with eight guest rooms set to be finished by spring 2011.

ABOVE The cozy living room at Swan House OPPOSITE, CLOCKWISE FROM TOP LEFT: A painted armoire in guestroom 1; Daisy; the discreet honesty bar; decorative windowpanes add charm and privacy to the guest room bathroom

GRAVETYE MANOR   EAST GRINSTEAD, WEST SUSSEX

*T*HE LONG DRIVEWAY to Gravetye Manor winds through thickening forest, passing a neighboring farm with chugging tractors and offering glimpses into the lush, surrounding pastureland, building adequate anticipation for the impending arrival. Occupying a generous plot of one thousand acres of forestry, the elegant Elizabethan manor house remains as stately as it was when built in 1598, commanding 360-degree views of the rolling hills and presiding over thirty-five acres of renowned historic gardens. Owned by the late William Robinson, a pioneer of England's Natural Garden, from 1884 to 1935, Gravetye Manor is well known for its glorious gardens, which now include a large kitchen garden. It was turned into a hotel in 1958 and has since garnered awards for its gardens and affiliation with Relais & Châteaux.

Despite the eighteen-room manor's considerable acreage and historic size, the atmosphere within is surprisingly unpretentious and relaxed. A sign outside the gravel carpark warns drivers to park in a front-facing direction, cheekily claiming that flowers don't take kindly to exhaust. The prevailing contrast between the estate's austere structure and its relaxed country ambiance is evident right from the entry's steep stone steps and ivy-covered portico. Through the massive wooden doors, the threshold is marked by a row of neatly lined-up wellies and walking sticks, while an oversized fresh floral arrangement, clearly collected from the gardens, sits on an antique carved bench, catching the eye and warming the staid Tudor oak-paneled main hall. The first

glimpse of furnishings includes all antique or inherited collectibles, some quite tired, yet altogether appropriate and ultimately comforting in their unstuffiness.

On the spacious ground floor, ancient mullioned windows, carved mantels, and various mismatched pieces of faded, upholstered period furniture complete the aesthetic of faded glory. Nevertheless, the décor maintains a sense of elegant timelessness, which propels guests to appreciate the palpable sense of history. Any sort of pretention involving the latest fad in high-end hotels or big-name interior designers is entirely lacking here. Instead, the intent is to show a renowned plot of the old English countryside, focusing on its exceptional gardens and woodland and treating guests to an enchanting evening immersed in it all. The main staircase of the house, with its carved railings, is a tribute to the building's stately origin, as are the polished paneled walls, carved ceilings, and arched doorways with curved wooden doors separating the upstairs hallways. The wooden floors provide the expected creaking of a historic manor house. One of Gravetye's finest points is, however, a contemporary addition: the daily floral arrangements. A talented team of four florists works tirelessly, cutting flowers from the expansive gardens and designing bouquets both small and large to adorn the various alcoves, antique tables, and wide windowsills of the old house. The pleasant arrangements infuse the house with vibrancy and assure the guest that things are indeed being looked after fastidiously.

The dining experience at Gravetye Manor earns high marks for being both professional and delicious. The kitchen garden supplies up to 95 percent of the fruits and vegetables during the summer, ensuring the freshest ingredients. At dinner, a charming young waitress from Germany, who was very knowledgeable about the menu, delivered her pronouncements on the dishes with poise and personality. A small tray of curiously diverse canapés—beef tartare, falafel bites in lentil bean dip, and smoked fish paté—arrived at the table, foreshadowing the variety of what was to come. The highlighted dish of local lamb is well worth sampling, as is the beef with crimini mushrooms and a rich wine sauce, which holds true to its description. The restaurant's wine list is extensive, with more than five hundred selections ranging from European wines to those of the New World. The intimate dining room (the largest table seats eight) is similarly traditional, with oak panels, a carved ceiling, gilded mirrors, white linen tablecloths, and classic, Queen Anne dining chairs. Weather permitting, lunch is served out on the stone patio overlooking the garden at either the umbrella tables or canvas seating areas. Given the historic house's lovely setting and convenient location just twelve miles from Gatwick Airport, dining here is quite popular and reservations must be made.

Despite the fineness of the food at lunch and dinner, breakfast was actually my favorite meal. It was quiet and relaxed, with just the right level of unobtrusive service for

the morning. My coffee cup was refilled twice without my asking, and the food arrived either piping hot or suitably chilled. Worth noting is Gravetye's new full-day menu, a rarity in staid hotels in England, which allows guests to order food at their whim and enjoy a less formal dining experience in the garden or one of the sitting rooms. With such service-oriented amenities as special dining in the garden's gazebo (which seats up to twelve), pre-made picnics (the more elaborate version includes wicker furniture), and customized walks for the super-active, Gravetye Manor has wisely kept on top of the demands of today's clientele without compromising its historic and authentic setting.

AUTHOR'S NOTE Since my visit, the manor was bought (in March 2010) by Londoner Jeremy Hosking, a hedge-fund manager and frequent guest who plans to revitalize the property and turn it into one of the leading country house hotels in England. He plans to begin his focus on restoring the gardens to their full potential and has brought in Tom Coward, the head gardener of the classic Great Dixter, who intends to bring about the garden's natural essence. He also maintains that any improvements made will be done with "great empathy towards the historic nature of the building."

ROOMS

The rooms at Gravetye Manor are, without hesitation, some of the more quintessentially English-style guest rooms you will find. Presumably untouched in the last twenty-five to thirty years, they are categorized by size: small, medium, and large. The large rooms are worth reserving, as the space helps promote the grandeur of the old house. Named after the various tree species found on the property, the rooms differ in color scheme and layout. Two of the top-floor rooms, Lime and Mulberry, are safe selections, affording great views, spacious bathrooms, and king-sized beds (two twins pushed together) that feel extra plush after a long garden walk. I prefer Mulberry, with its slanted attic walls, darling corner vanity with chintz skirt, and plush pink carpet—a wonderful throwback and cozy environment despite the 432-square-foot space. A few contemporary surprises abound, like fast WiFi in all the rooms, updated showerheads, and generously sized bottles of Molten Brown products. One of the large rooms, known as the Master Bedroom, is a standout, with pale green wall-to-wall carpeting, oak-paneled walls, a prestigious corner position with two sides of mullioned windows, and antique furniture including a gorgeous sixteenth-century chest. Purposely antiquated, the room has a carved mantel framed on either side by two vestiges of the home's original owners and a four-poster queen-sized Tudor bed with thick floral drapery. The views from the windows carry over the gardens and into the valley. The bathroom of the Master Bedroom is a complete departure from the traditionally styled room, decorated in a zany, Art Deco style, with aqua-colored tiles and matching porcelain fixtures. The wall-to-wall carpeting and absence of a shower may be difficult to endure for those accustomed to more modern bathroom appointments; however, those looking to try something a bit eccentric (it *is* England, after all) will be delighted.

OPPOSITE, CLOCKWISE FROM TOP LEFT The oak-paneled lobby; an enormous gilded mirror befitting the room's grand dimensions; wellies and walking sticks by the front door; the Master Bedroom's traditional floral print ABOVE The stone cut courtyard leading out to the ample property surrounding Gravetye Manor

HARTWELL HOUSE AYLESBURY, BUCKINGHAMSHIRE

ONE OF ENGLAND'S remaining seventeenth-century, stately homes with a pedigree that includes a mention in the Doomsday Book and such notable former residents as Louis XVIII, the exiled king of France, Hartwell House offers a dramatic and intimate vantage of the way England's historic gentry once lived. The Grade I–listed house is set in ninety acres of luscious parkland laid out by a contemporary of Lancelot "Capability" Brown and characterized by a swan-filled lake spanned by stone bridges, eighteenth-century statues, a deconsecrated church, and neighboring cow pastures. Just forty-five minutes from London, in rural Buckinghamshire, Hartwell House underwent a complete refurbishment from 1989 to 1992 and since 2008 has been owned and managed by the National Trust. Retaining original features of both Jacobean and Georgian architectural and design influences, including decorative paneling and ceilings, priceless art, and antique furnishings, the thirty-bedroom mansion will delight English history and design aficionados. If the grand statue of Frederick, Prince of Wales, on horseback at the hotel's circular drive didn't quite alert you to the house's prestige, the golden stone exterior with its Jacobean round-arched arcades and majestic, early eighteenth-century Great Hall entrance certainly will.

Given its stature, Hartwell House is frequently visited upon by tourists and historical purveyors and in return is open to the public for dining and afternoon tea—a particularly elaborate affair, with a wide array of homemade tea sandwiches, scones, and decadent pastries like lemon sponge and fruit tart. Its immense popularity makes reservations, no matter if you're an in-house guest, a must. Tea reservations are also specified by location and I highly recommend soliciting spots in either in the light-filled drawing room under the intricately carved ceiling, on the back stone patio overlooking the manicured south lawn with its William II Obelisk, or in the eighteenth-century library in front of the marble fireplace and richly decorated Rococo plasterwork.

Filled with historic lore (King Louis XVIII of France learned he was reinstated as king here) and frequent host to contemporary leaders (President Clinton, the emperor and empress of Japan), Hartwell House maintains a palpable, dignified air today, equally confident in its past eminence and current distinction above other country hotels. The superior attitude is clear right upon check-in, when the kindly butler whisks your luggage to your room and the desk clerk insists upon touring you around the impressive ground floor before showing you to your room. I recommend acquiescing and then confirming your dinner and tea reservations.

Offering forty-six rooms—thirty in the main house and sixteen in Hartwell Court, the newly converted eighteenth-century indoor riding center and stables—Hartwell House appeals to guests looking for a short country escape that is filled with historic prominence, elegant dining, and leisure afforded by the surrounding greenery, tennis courts, and spa. Outfitted with a large indoor pool, full gym, steam and sauna rooms, spa bath, and four treatment rooms, the Hartwell Spa is a wonderful modern addition to the otherwise antique space. Again, though, this space is open to the public through club memberships and therefore has a limited sense of exclusivity. Hartwell Court also offers a casual dining space overlooking the indoor pool should a more informal meal be necessary.

Given the striking preservation, Hartwell House offers a stunning backdrop for a special event or wedding, with priceless photo opportunities in the eighteenth-century Hartwell Church, the antique stone bridge that hails from the original Kew Bridge in London, and the south lawn's well-groomed topiaries. A distinct destination guaranteed to set your eighteenth-century fantasies afloat, Hartwell House merits a visit on superficial reasons—the chance to stay in a preserved English mansion—alone.

ROOMS

Climbing the stupendous Gothic staircase, with its Jacobean carved figures along the banister, sets the stage for the following three floors of guest rooms in the main house. Each room or suite is decorated individually with matching chintz and bedspreads, antique Elizabethan furnishings, fine art on the walls, and plush carpeting that keeps the English chill at bay. Views from the rooms also differ. I highly

PAGES 110–11 The property's historic footbridge with stone originating from London's Kew Bridge PREVIOUS PAGES The south lawn with the shadow of the obelisk ABOVE The cushioned window seats of the Queen's Room OPPOSITE The sumptuous bedroom of the Lee suite

recommend booking a south lawn–facing room for the most light and a placid, verdant view. I'm partial to the Royal Four-Poster suites—the King's and Queen's rooms— given their sense of history, grand dimensions (both are corner suites), period furniture, and king-sized four-poster beds. The Queen's Room is particularly alluring, with a feminine pink-and-green floral chintz, an antique secretary desk, and cushioned window seats offering pleasing vistas of the south lawn topiaries, the swans on the lake, and even the cows grazing beyond. While staying there, I was treated to a delightful summer thunderstorm (the telltale signs being the neighboring cows sitting down, of course) and fell into a cozy, sedated state curled up with my book among the silk pillows buffeting the window ledge. The canopy bed was deliciously plush, with finely pressed sheets and copious down pillows. Don't let the chintz fool you—the room is well furnished with modern comforts, such as flat-screen TVs , DVD players, and WiFi. Despite the bathroom's cramped dimensions—particularly given the large-

ness of the bedroom—I was perfectly soothed by a soak in the tub with the brass fixtures' strong pressure, Penhaligons products, and framed view of the lawn.

My second choice is the grand Lee suite, the largest room at Hartwell House. Overlooking the south lawn's landscaped gardens with a generously sized sitting room separated from the bedroom by an internal hallway, the room is ideal for longer-staying guests or those with business. The king-sized bedroom has a pleasing décor with a butter-yellow and blue rosette wallpaper, cream-colored bedspread, and antique porcelain lamps, while the sitting room feels stronger and more masculine with Regency gold-and-green-striped wallpaper, ornate plasterwork on the moldings, and gilt-framed oils of the Lee family, former owners of the house, credited with the topiary garden design in 1609. As expected, the guest rooms in the main house are far more evocative of the house's esteemed origins than those in the newer, Hartwell Court wing. However, if you plan to bring your furry friend or small children, the Gallery and Court suites in Hartwell Court

have private garden entrances and spacious, duplex-style layouts. And if your main intent is to utilize the spa and its casual dining café, then again, the Hartwell Court rooms make more sense. A final accommodation option best suited for groups or a longer-staying family is the recently renovated Rectory building, which sleeps seven. Tucked behind the eighteenth-century church and across the winding driveway from Hartwell Court, the typical Georgian country house features a large backyard with a private outdoor swimming pool. English country style is readily dispersed through the house, with chintz-covered bedrooms, wall-to-wall carpeting, and cozy sitting rooms with rocking chairs and built-in shelves. Despite the modern offerings of Hartwell Court or the added privacy of the Rectory, I find that the true heart of Hartwell House, and the very reason behind visiting, is its impressive historic preservation. Thus staying in one of the classically appointed rooms in the main house is the best bet for guests to appreciate the essence of this distinct and distinguished property.

ABOVE Frederick, Prince of Wales, on horseback OPPOSITE, CLOCKWISE FROM TOP LEFT The eighteenth-century Rococo fireplace in the library; the ornate, Victorian-style drawing room; freestanding candelabras add to the historic appeal of Hartwell House; bay window seating overlooking the south lawn

AUGILL CASTLE
KIRKBY STEPHEN, CUMBRIA

*J*UST PAST THE small village of Kirkby Stephen on the edge of the beloved Lake District, Augill Castle sits regally nestled into the lush, rolling hillside. Despite the soaring stone turrets, traditional castle balustrade, and massive framed glass windows, it is as unassuming as a castle can be. Built in 1837 by a gentleman who wished to entertain his friends and family in a refined setting, the castle has been in private hands ever since. Not without a colorful history, Augill Castle has played host to notable figures since the early nineteenth century. Chief among them was Doctor Abercrombie, surgeon to Queen Victoria and French Canadian airmen during World War II. Since then, the house suffered through various stages of disrepair, neglect, and poor development ideas (it was subdivided into apartments) until 1997, when Wendy and Simon Bennet purchased the castle. Today, the Bennets run the castle as a modern and surprisingly casual bed-and-breakfast, trumpeting the property with the tantalizing tagline "stay in a castle." Such advertisement seems to offer guests the rare chance to live like nobility, though it is a simple statement of fact, and this castle actually presents a casual, home-style persona totally absent of grandeur and formality.

The entrance is marked by a small brown sign that leads the guest down the castle's unadorned gravel and grass driveway, past a small pond, a well-used children's swing set, and a worn tennis court. The familial entrance makes pulling up to the Victorian castle a wonderful study in contrast. Towering over the flat gravel entry, the light-colored stone castle with its ivy-covered, arched wooden door casts quite an impressive shadow over its new arrivals. Fortunately a small, framed sign on the door directs guests to ring the bell; otherwise guests might stand idle, gawking at the quiet magnificence around them. The sign also says to ring the bell twice if need be, stating rather congenially that it may take a while for someone to come. The absence of a doorman or butler sets the casual, almost irreverent tone of the domicile's architectural stature.

Leather-bound guest books, found in the rooms, offer an introduction to the castle along with the Bennets' renovation story. The first bit reads like a disclaimer, stating plainly that the owners hope you have not arrived under any false pretenses and promising to offer the same services as a hotel despite their casual attitude. It goes on to declare that there is "no uniformed staff, no fancy leisure facilities, no regimented timetable for check in, check-out, or breakfast." The second part details, in candid fashion, how the Bennets risked much to open the castle as a bed-and-breakfast, debated selling a few times over the past fourteen years, are raising their two small children on the premises, and generally feel as though they have achieved a lot. The myriad commendations, including national awards such as the Best Bed & Breakfast in Britain in 2008 and finalist for the Best UK Boutique Hotel, no doubt confirm that.

The castle's interior retains elements of its former physique—massive dimen-sions, elegant corbels, and wide stone fireplaces—alongside the effects of a contemporary young family. Atop a beautiful carved wooden cupboard in the front parlor sits a ceramic plate, a framed picture of a small dog, and a children's glittery star wand. Some rooms appear more majestic than others, like the blue dining room featuring a carved, painted ceiling and a long, twenty-person table that hosts family-style breakfast in the mornings and four-course meals on Friday and Saturday evenings (plus special events). In the cozy foyer you'll find a cracked leather sofa, a harlequin design on the mantel of the fireplace, and a hodge-podge of antique furnishings. Tall, arched doorways frame each ground-floor room, while bold, rich colors adorn the walls, calling attention to the castle's impressive dimensions.

The grounds of the castle are a true highlight for children and adults alike. The front lawn features a quaint stone terrace and circular bench area planted with an herbaceous border reminiscent of the popular style of the Victorian era. Given the climate up in the north of the country, there are few tender plants in the garden, although Wendy and Simon do nurture bountiful potted geraniums and the lawn's front slope is festooned with colorful semiwild flowers and thick meadow grass. The west lawn is home to free-range chickens whose eggs help supply breakfast and very presence lend to the bucolic nature of the castle's surroundings. Indeed, the delight of Augill Castle is in its distinctive dual identity as both a

castle and a laid-back, family-oriented bed-and-breakfast. The neighboring farmland, with herds of sheep and cows, is a delightful bonus for those looking to explore the local land, while I highly recommend taking a long walk (Holly, the gentle Labrador, may even accompany you) eastward, heading uphill toward North Stainmore, so you can view the beautiful northern countryside and its plotted drystone walls from high vantage. The vista is all-encompassing and wonderfully English. However, the best part may just be trotting downhill, back to your private castle for the evening.

ROOMS

As the property's literature clearly states, "Augill Castle is not a conventional hotel, but a family home which welcomes guests." And indeed the fourteen guest rooms are anything but conventional hotel-style accommodations. Similar to a personal home, each room bears its own unique character, making it easy to choose a favorite. Decorated by Wendy, all the rooms exhibit a certain quirkiness mixed in with the traditional furnishings. With a penchant for antique appliances and housewares, Wendy has littered both the upstairs hallway and the guest rooms with such relics as antique sewing machines, church pews, and typewriters, along with vintage curios: hand-bound books, Victorian-era prints, and brass-plated button light switches. Each room features a tempting tea and coffee tray with homemade cookies and a bottle of sherry with two crystal glasses. Augill Castle's kid-friendliness includes the availability of children's toys, as well as a ready supply of baby monitors and food purees.

Given the varying sizes and styles of the individual rooms—some have four-poster beds, others stained-glass windows or wardrobes fashioned from the turret walls—it is wise to be as specific as possible about a request when booking. Wendy promises that although the rooms are colorfully adorned, there is absolutely no chintz, and they all boast fine Egyptian cotton linen, fluffy towels, and satellite television. A small framed picture of each room as it was when Wendy and Simon first found it offers a remarkably endearing, if not encouraging, before-and-after perspective

The Haygarth Room occupies the prestigious location over the front portico and features a massive, iron-mullioned window framed by tufted orange silk curtains. The king-sized sleigh bed is a tad springy, but the sheets, as promised, are crisp and comfortable. Waking up to streaming sunlight and the view down the grassy front lawn and pastures beyond is pleasantly comforting and may very well keep you in bed longer than usual. The castle's top room and perpetual crowd-pleaser, Pendragon, is a sure-fire stunner. Although its bathroom is quite narrow and has just one vanity and a cramped shower, the room's oversized, King Henry four-poster bed compensates for any residual discomfort. Set in the middle of the room between two opposing walls of full-length windows and facing the ornately carved mantel and its working fireplace, the bed delivers the appropriate feeling of grandeur you'd expect from your night in a castle. A less dramatic, though no less enchanting, option is Langdale, with its delicate blue-and-white floral wallpaper, antique four-poster bed, and charming embroidered duvet.

Be forewarned that located directly behind the castle there are three simple row houses belonging to private individuals not affiliated with the hotel. The residents are quiet and appear to keep to themselves, though guests are asked not to walk behind the castle. The rooms facing the back of the castle look over these houses and the small parking area behind it, so it's best to request a front-facing view. The castle also features a family suite tucked back between one of the permanent residents' homes and the castle. The suite has two bedrooms and plenty of space for vacationing families, though my recommendation, and the evident reason behind visiting Augill, is to spend the night in the castle so you can gleefully check castle-dwelling off your list of things to do.

OPPOSITE, CLOCKWISE FROM TOP LEFT A gramophone and stained-glass windows add to the charm; abundant wood carvings decorate doors and furnishings; the bright primary tones of the ground floor interiors; the secluded guest suite ABOVE The master suite with its bed set center stage

YOREBRIDGE HOUSE NORTH YORKSHIRE

*L*OCATED IN THE Yorkshire Dales—northern England's upland area known for its massive national park, flowing river valleys, and rolling hills—Yorebridge House provides the ultimate stopover in one of the country's more breathtaking spots. Characterized by bright green pastureland divided by England's signature drystone walls and littered with grazing sheep and cattle, the Dales, usually U- or V-shaped valleys, are favored for their bucolic scenery, horseback riding, cycling, and heather moorland ideal for grouse shooting.

As a result, journeying to the remote Yorebridge House, a former schoolmaster's house nestled alongside the flowing river Ure, feels a bit like a pilgrimage to a faraway land. Fortunately the scenery, as well as the small, eleven-bedroom hotel and restaurant, offer an immediate reward. Acquired by Charlotte and David Reilly in September 2006, the Victorian house, accompanying stable, and garden grounds have undergone complete renovations in order to create this luxury boutique property. The passionate young couple poured their hearts, souls, and professional skills (David was a salesman at Bang & Olufsen and Charlotte ran her own design firm) into the creation of Yorebridge House, with special focus on food, wine, inspiring interiors, and relaxation amid the peaceful countryside.

As you step inside the eighteenth-century stone house, the full-blown refurbishment is eminently clear, generously lit by the tall Georgian windows. Polished floors meet whitewashed walls and modern light fixtures, while casual, contemporary furnishings like square leather chairs and bright red ottomans decorate the sitting room. Adam, the front manager, instinctively understands that guests much prefer to be shown their rooms rather than exchange lengthy pleasantries upon arrival. The ground floor consists of two sitting rooms, a corner lounge with metallic wallpaper, and a refurbished bar area that indeed welcomes many. With seating for twenty-two, a polished design, and a fresh menu that includes treats such as pumpkin and parmesan risotto, seared trout, and a delicious Yorkshire Ploughman's lunch, the bar is a popular venue, frequently buzzing with visitors and locals alike.

Highly lauded, the contemporary-style restaurant at Yorebridge House is one of the hotel's main assets. Open for lunch and dinner and already a favorite among the locals (which include residents within a sixty-mile radius), the thirty-seat establishment prides itself on using only the freshest of ingredients with inventive, gourmet-style preparation (somewhat unexpected out in the Dales). Amid the potted palms, head chef James Fiske is gunning for a Michelin star with such stunningly rich dishes as langoustine and lobster ravioli, local lamb and rosemary sausage, and red-wine-poached halibut that there's little question to the restaurant's favorable reputation. Desserts are a must, with the standout *asiette* of chocolate that will put any chocolate lover in a delighted state of ecstasy. David's passion for wine is reflected in the extensive wine list, featuring bottles from both Europe and abroad. If David is there (which is often), he will happily suggest bottles from his cellar, and my advice is to listen: his taste and knowledge are impressive.

Given the surrounding natural beauty, fall is one of the best times to visit, when the colors are rich and saturated, making long walks in the Dales picturesque. Of course, the snow-covered landscape is quite stunning too, though beware, you may end up staying longer than you intended. Despite its small size and out-of-the-way location, Yorebridge House delivers all the same service requisites as a larger, urban hotel yet with the intimate touch of a boutique property. Both Charlotte and David clearly understand how to offer luxury in a sophisticated manner, making hibernating in this remote location serene and comforting.

ROOMS

The eleven rooms at Yorebridge House differ extensively, with no two alike. Decorated by Charlotte with individual themes based on travel experiences or specific places, the guest rooms at Yorebridge all seek to offer a transporting and escapist experience for the guest. All of the rooms feature top-quality Bang & Olufsen televisions and radios, while Charlotte's sensitive interior design affords the rooms a thoughtful décor, which greatly affects the guests' stay, as does the chilled wine and extensive DVD selection. Seven of the eleven rooms in the main house and converted riverside stables are suites and are

PAGE 122 Victorian wood panels used as a headboard in Carabeo, one of the guest rooms overlooking the river OPPOSITE The former schoolhouse's delightful symmetry ABOVE The river Ure FOLLOWING PAGE LEFT A freestanding tub under a crystal chandelier in the Pienza guest room FOLLOWING PAGE RIGHT, CLOCKWISE FROM TOP LEFT Classic minimalist design at Yorebridge House; the simple yet delicious restaurant; masculine tones in the lounge; the boudoir style of Pienza

easily the preferred locations in the hotel. My top choice in the main house is Pienza, the Italian-style room named after the Tuscan city. Decorated in deep grays with Osborne & Little wallpaper, elegantly carved furniture, crystal chandeliers, and a roll-top bath deviously located in the corner of the bedroom, Pienza caters to romantics looking to unwind. The tall Georgian windows offer clear views of the Dales, while the modern

bathroom has a walk-in shower, a sleek marble-topped vanity, and Molten Brown products. Another favorite is the oft-requested Bainbridge suite, with its spacious marble-floor bathroom and corner setting. In the stables, I am partial to St. Jean, the Caribbean room whose private terrace and hot tub overlooking the gushing river continue the island theme. The bright, airy room includes a light oak four-poster bed,

muslin curtains, and simple whitewashed walls with framed island prints. An updated bathroom has mosaic tile and a slipper tub. Of course, falling asleep to the sonorous track of streaming water is the ultimate experience in relaxation. I highly recommend ordering breakfast to the room, as it is wonderfully prepared and arrives piping hot—and the beds are comfy enough to indulge such extravagant behavior.

A CORNER OF EDEN Kirkby Stephen, Cumbria

*S*ECLUDED, QUIET, AND surrounded solely by livestock from the two neighboring farms and ruins from an old castle, A Corner of Eden is most appropriately named for those with solitary tendencies. Truly a spot where you can hole up in the bucolic countryside and set your days by the hours of sunlight, this charming bed-and-breakfast allows visitors to turn back the clock on modernity and be swept away by the richness of the land.

The eighteenth-century, four-bedroom, Grade II–listed farmhouse sits tucked into the Eden Valley between Cumbria and Yorkshire counties and is reached by turning off a nondescript farm road and following a winding gravel driveway. Owners Debbie and Richard Temple bought the property, which includes the main house and two separate farmhouses, three years ago and fastidiously renovated it themselves. A photo album in the drawing room showcases the dramatic transformation of the house, including the restoration of the old oak doors and furniture, the wallpapering of guest rooms, the ripping up of waterlogged floors, and the recycling of old stone for the guest rooms' fireplaces.

Upon every guest's arrival, Debbie lights a fire in the drawing room—no matter the season—and stocks the butler's pantry with farm-fresh delicacies. Despite its naturally cool temperature, thanks to slate-topped countertops, oak walls, and a stone floor, the pantry is the most-occupied spot in the house. And with good reason! Shelves are lined with Debbie's homemade chutneys and Richard's black currant sloe gin, along-

side dried mushrooms, fruit-flavored teacakes, and a platter of local cheese and homemade bread. Open all day for guests to help themselves, the pantry also features plenty of drinks (sodas, beers, liquor, and wine), multiple teakettles (this is England, after all), cafétières for coffee, and bowls of nuts and fruit for the quick nibble. Meticulously restocked by Debbie throughout the day, the pantry represents the heart and soul of A Corner of Eden, melding the old with the fresh offerings of today.

Eating well at A Corner of Eden is practically guaranteed. Every meal served, from breakfast to the preset menus at dinner, features homemade chutneys, bread, and cakes, while the produce comes straight from Debbie's impressive vegetable garden. Her green thumb is so prodigious that seven out of ten items in each meal come directly from the garden, including spring onions, lettuce, new potatoes, tomatoes, pumpkins, beetroot, garlic, zucchini, sweet peas, carrots, rhubarb, strawberries, and eggplant. She will happily pass along any recipes, though for the sake of your waistline, the instructions for shortbread squares with dark chocolate tops should remain in the fields of Cumbria.

Multiple sets of wellies and Barbour jackets are available for guests so that they may traverse the many miles of surrounding walking trails, including a few steep hikes and even a cut path that leads directly to the local pub. Ask about the cupboard filled with board games and books, from area guides to novels, as well as a map of local walks with lines drawn directly from the front door of

A Corner of Eden. The area is also the most northerly point of the Pennine Bridleway and is thus surrounded by excellent open riding country.

Richard is an accomplished carpenter, having crafted the gorgeous dining room table from a local oak tree. The bedside tables, guest room armoires, and various carved adornments around the house are also fine examples of Richard's handiwork.

As with the interior of the house, the grounds are treated with the utmost care. Amid the grassy fields and drystone walls is a small pond and a stone patio filled with comfortable teak furniture and chaises. Ideal for napping and dining alfresco, the patio is colorfully decorated with pots of perennials, rose bushes, and even the occasional pecking chicken. Every morning a fire is lit in the dining room, lending a comforting, old-fashioned ambiance to the day. Add to that the simple soundtrack of braying sheep and wind rustling in the trees, and it's as if you've been transported eighty years back in time.

ROOMS

Organized as a bed-and-breakfast with four separate rooms (though only two bathrooms, since historic-building restrictions forbid the addition of en suite facilities), A Corner of Eden is best suited for exclusive use among friends or family, with Debbie onsite as the ever-conscientious hostess and lauded cook (her local baking awards are on display in the butler's pantry). Of course those accustomed to traditional bed-and-

breakfasts, where sharing a bathroom with strangers is not the least bit uncomfortable, will be perfectly happy at A Corner of Eden.

Located upstairs, the four bedrooms fan out from the second-floor landing, with two bathrooms featuring showers and toilets. One bathroom features a cast-iron bathtub, the view from which is textbook English countryside. The large glass window, located right over the square-shaped sink, overlooks the sheep- and cow-filled fields and undulating lines of the drystone walls. This picturesque view can also be seen from a glorious church window off the center staircase. A generous window seat brims with pillows, while the wall-length glass allows ample light throughout the back of the house.

Three of the four guest rooms feature double beds, while the fourth offers two twins and an appealing color scheme of creams and browns. Each of the bedrooms features brocade or satin jewel-toned quilts on the beds, which appear heavy in the summer but cozy for the fall and winter. Two of the double rooms have iron beds (one is a four-poster), while the third has a carved-wood bed, which has the firmest mattress of the lot and a cream satin embroidered bedcover. Unlike rooms at the more contemporary-style guesthouses dotting the countryside, those at A Corner of Eden reflect the house's and its owners' DIY roots. Absent of ubiquitous luxury trimmings such as Italian linens and marble bathrooms with name-brand bath products, the amenities at A Corner of Eden are homegrown, like the carafes of Richard's sloe gin in the rooms and complimentary toiletry bags of freshly scented creams and shampoos packed and assembled by Debbie herself. The landing and mid-century staircase are covered with a plum-colored carpet (a seemingly popular and unique-to-England color choice), though the floors of the rooms have been wisely left bare to highlight the recently

refurbished oak flooring. The abundance of locally harvested oak—from furniture to reclaimed paneling on the guest room window seats—give the interiors a rich, homey feel, which enhances the authenticity of the place. Being a guest and waking up each day at A Corner of Eden is bound to feel other-worldly, simply because it is.

ꜰᴏᴘᴘᴏꜱɪᴛᴇ The twin-bed guest room's chocolate colored palette and backyard view making it one of the most appealing rooms in the house ᴏᴘᴘᴏꜱɪᴛᴇ, ᴄʟᴏᴄᴋᴡɪꜱᴇ ꜰʀᴏᴍ ᴛᴏᴘ ʟᴇꜰᴛ The beloved butler's pantry with home-cooked wares; farm-fresh eggs; the staid, country style ᴇ double guest room; the ever-burning dining room fireplace

Our girls'
Free Range Eggs

HAMBLETON HALL HOTEL OAKHAM, RUTLAND

*J*UST TWO HOURS outside London, Hambleton Hall Hotel is arguably one of Britain's most ideally situated manor homes. Cresting the top of a finely groomed hill, the house overlooks Western Europe's largest man-made lake, Rutland Water, the result of a purposeful flooding of the lower lands in the late 1970s. Rutland Water Reservoir horseshoes around what is now known as Hambleton Peninsula, where the century-old Hambleton Hall is the crown jewel, enjoying 270-degree views of lapping water.

Built it 1881 by brewery magnate Walter Marshall as a fox-hunting lodge, Hambleton Hall features classic Victorian architecture, with a gray stone façade, mullioned windows, and multiple gables. However, it didn't grow into its beauty until 1979, when the current owners, Tim and Stefa Hart, transformed the property into a sophisticated country-house hotel with seventeen guest rooms and a gourmet restaurant, earning it the prestigious Relais & Châteaux affiliation.

Stepping through the hotel's antique stone portico, complete with overhead Latin inscription, somehow feels deliciously familiar, as though your period dream of arriving to your English manor house has suddenly come true. The pleasing interior décor, overseen by Stefa, who owns her own decorating firm, is of a traditional style, with cream-colored wallpaper, buillon fringe on the silk drapery, watercolors in gilded frames, arched beamed ceilings, and a charming paneled staircase. Composed of three main sitting rooms, each with a fire-place, the ground floor feels enchantingly English, from the intimate, masculine bar with horse-and-hound oil paintings and leather furnishings to the eye-catching, French-inspired drawing room with embroidered fabrics like Claremont's Les Raisins, Pierre Frey Orsay velvet, and Lelievre velvet Mogador, elegant crown moldings, and a ornamental ceiling. A lovely bay window is framed by Percheron curtains with Hermitage trimmings, and two sets of French doors open to the stone terrace, showcasing the sparkling water view. Given the heavy traffic in the drawing room—cocktails and canapés are served here in the evenings— each year the room gets some form of an update, from reupholstery to reapplications of the hand-painted wallpaper from George Spencer. What sold me, however, was the massive arrangement of lilies, alstroemerias, and delphiniums from the garden towering upon the walnut console table. The bright and airy room is just the complement to the intimate, denlike bar.

Renowned for its fine dining, Hambleton Hall's restaurant is headed by Michelin-starred chef Aaron Patterson. Offering local produce and game whenever possible, the menu is seasonal, featuring truffles in January followed by asparagus, lettuce, and herbs from the kitchen garden and local fowl such as grouse, partridge, and woodcock. The exceptional wine list is best sampled through the guidance of the kind sommelier, Dominique. The tasting menu was superb, particularly the duck entrée, expertly paired with a New Zealand merlot, and the desserts are not to be missed, especially the weekly-changing soufflés (if it's passion fruit, you're in luck). The room's setting is delightfully intimate, due to its signature odd angles and corners, while the views from the grand bay windows and the tucked-away tables for two offer a sense of romance. Adorned with a striking Regency striped wallpaper, special-ordered from Coles, and rich red walls in another, the room is demonstrably warm and engaging, especially at night, when silver candelabras complete the traditional mise-en-scène. The restaurant is popular with the locals, and private dinner parties are a constant, so be sure to let the hotel know when you plan to dine in-house.

Surrounded by manicured gardens overlooking 276 acres of parkland, the hotel's immediate grounds include a lovely heated pool surrounded by an attractive ivy-covered brick wall and teak lounge chairs, a croquet lawn, and a tennis court. At the bottom of the property's hill is a gated entrance onto the gravel bridle path located right at the water's edge. The five-mile peninsula path skirts the water and then continues onto the road and back through the area's surrounding forest and farmland. It provides an excellent route for jogging or biking and is also the launch point for kayaking or sailing; just be sure to study the map prior to setting off. Rutland Water offers no shortage of activities, and owner Tim Hart's complimentary booklet of things to do in the area, including visiting local market towns with antique shops, art galleries, and museums, ensures that guests at Hambleton Hall Hotel can take full advantage of their venue.

PAGE 134 The Gothic entrance of Hambleton Hall Hotel OPPOSITE Sitting room of the appropriately titled Blue Room
ABOVE The manicured gardens and sloping view down to Rutland Water FOLLOWING PAGES Classic Victorian elegance at Hambleton Hall Hotel

ROOMS

The guest rooms at Hambleton Hall have the same level of detailed and thoughtful décor as the ground floor, including traditional elements and fine fabrics. Overseen by Stefa, each of the seventeen guest rooms is uniquely decorated, with clever names that pinpoint their various characteristics. The two-bedroom Croquet Pavilion is separated from the main house by the croquet lawn (hence the name) and, with its own breakfast room and two spacious guest rooms and bathrooms, is an ideal option for a family. The rest of the rooms are on the second, third, and fourth floors of the main house. One of my favorites, Lotus, located on the top floor, offers sky-grazing views of the luscious gardens, stone terrace and glittering lake. The room, with angled eaves, has been made delightfully snug by the feminine Manuel Canovas cornflower-blue and cream Pali wallpaper and matching chintz. Two linen-covered cushioned chairs with blue piping occupy the room's corners, while a retro ivory-colored art deco vanity table covered in faux-crocodile-skin glamorizes the space. The wall-length closet wisely features full-length mirror panels, appeasing female guests everywhere, while the bathroom has been freshly updated with a circular mirror and shower/tub combination that feels roomy despite the bathroom's narrow eaves. With perhaps the softest cotton sheets I found throughout England, the king-sized bed, with its embroidered coverlet, was not only classically elegant but also dangerously comfortable. I highly suggest ordering tea or coffee to your room each morning to delay the eventual exit from bed.

Other top choices that also feature the prized lakeside view include the Fern Room, with its antique canopy bed, bay window, and delicate green-stenciled walls; the Blue Room, with its deep blue linen walls by Osborne and Little and streaming morning light; and the red Qazvin Room, embellished with seventeenth-century hand-painted Persian panels that the Harts found in Iran on their honeymoon. If all the lake-view rooms are taken, then I suggest the somewhat cramped, yet undeniably special Noel Coward Room on the second floor. Its bold color scheme has Nina Campbell's bright purple and green "clianthus" fabric on the walls and curtains juxtaposed with a lime-green headboard. The bathroom offers plenty of space and framed photographs of Coward, a frequent Hambleton Hall guest himself. Some rooms feature more updated technology and more recently renovated bathrooms, but all have bathtub-shower combinations and the full range of Penhaligons products. Those seeking privacy should book the tangential cottage, which during my entire stay never gave its guests reason to emerge.

ABOVE The appealing color scheme of the Blue Room OPPOSITE, CLOCKWISE FROM TOP LEFT The cozy firelit bar; the sitting room, which gets reupholstered each year; the delicate style of the Lotus Room; a romantic corner table in the restaurant

SHARROW BAY COUNTRY HOUSE HOTEL Penrith, Cumbria

Arriving at Sharrow Bay Country House Hotel on Ullswater Lake in England's beloved Lake District provides perhaps one of the most awe-inspiring glimpses of England's surprisingly varied topography. The curvaceous mountaintop road known as the Kirkstone Pass, which begins at the top of Lake Windermere, the district's most popular and largest lake, offers easily the most memorable vistas of England, including the only sighting of bona fide mountains. All too often, visitors stick to the tourist haven of Lake Windermere, with its myriad activities, but I implore you to continue on, particularly toward Ullswater, which will reward you with bucolic scenery like grazing sheep, horses in paddocks, rocky walking trails, and antique steamers crossing the lake that once inspired Wordsworth. Here you will also find Sharrow Bay Country House Hotel, England's first-ever Relais & Châteaux dining and lodging establishment.

Completely devoid of modern updates (and such telltale amenities as WiFi, flat-screen televisions, and rain showers), the sixty-year-old country-house hotel retains its original pastoral character, albeit with some signature décor emblematic of its late owners. Governed by the personable Francis Coulson and Brian Sack (and later joined by Nigel Lightburn) for more than thirty years, the twenty-seven-room Sharrow Bay is a veritable showcase of their eclectic style (velveteen armchairs, pink wall-to-wall carpeting, and fringed everything) and love of antique curios, making guests feel as if they've been invited into a deeply personal space that just happens to offer one of England's most coveted lakeside views. Sadly, the charming gentlemen hosts (Coulson was known to compose nightly beside poems for guests) have passed, and the upkeep of the unique hotel rests upon the shoulders of the long-standing staff and new owners, the formidable Von Essen Group.

The spacious and deliciously secluded rooms are divided among four separate dwellings, from the eight king-sized chintz rooms in the main house to the six stand-alone garden rooms, to the four-bedroom Edwardian Gate House and five-bedroom Bank House, or "crown jewel," as it is referred to. You can spend your days trying the multiple walking paths found right outside the door, boarding the lake's two steamers, taking a helicopter tour, or nestling into one of the numerable lounge chairs or benches with a good book.

Retaining a Michelin star for more than a decade, Sharrow Bay offers a dining experience that continues to showcase a traditional home-style essence. The evening meal begins in typical Relais & Châteaux fashion with drinks and canapés served in the handsome front lounge with a roaring fire and a large picture window, whose view is so intimate the glass seems to be touching the lapping lake. Dinner is then served in the dining room, whose carpeted floors, heavy silk drapery framing the lake views, and antique English upholstered armchairs appear to have been untouched for the last thirty years. The locally infused menu features dishes like dressed crab with sautéed scallops and mango salsa and medallion of local venison, braised red cabbage, and apple and raisin, butternut squash purée. Sticky toffee pudding, which is purported to have been founded at Sharrow Bay, is instead called Francis's original icky sticky toffee sponge; served with cream or ice cream, it is sheer pleasure for even the most devout toffee pudding fan. The seven-hundred-bottle wine list has wines from all over the globe (and the prices to match). Be sure to request one of the tables in the windows, which allow the lakeside view to feel deliciously personal.

Despite the hotel's culinary prowess, there is a wonderful absence of stuffiness in the dining room and hotel overall. Even without the bubbly personality of the former owners, the idea behind Sharrow Bay remains about pure relaxation, and the prevailing attitude among the staff is to comfort guests far more than wow them—just as Brian and Francis taught them, in "the gentle art of Sharrow."

ROOMS

For the most private experience at Sharrow Bay, book the white-stone Bank House, situated just a mile down the road from the main house and overlooking the lake from a slightly elevated position. Built in the seventeenth century, this farmhouse was converted into a private home in the 1930s and has been part of the hotel since 1975. Accessed by a separate driveway, the Bank House provides ultimate seclusion and

PAGE 142 The cream-colored façade of the Bank House ABOVE Teddy bears decorate each of the guest rooms at the Bank House; Victorian-inspired interiors at the Bank House OPPOSITE The Portland-stone fireplace originating from Warwick Castle FOLLOWING PAGES The calm waters of Sharrow Bay

direct communication with the serenity of the lake. The house has five double bedrooms, all with en suite bathrooms and their own color scheme of chintz, a refectory dining room, and light blue and pink damask-covered lounges. Filled with Brian and Francis's signature style and antique finds—like incomplete Queen Anne tea sets, medieval pieces of armor, and early-century copper canisters—the Bank House delivers ambiance with full English tilt. The dining room is perhaps the most curious space, with a massive Portland-stone fireplace and carved mantel originating from Warwick Castle, plus rouge damask curtains and a carpet custom-made to resemble the

one in the Royal Opera House. Upholstered chairs with floral embroidery and fringe trim and wood-framed Tudor-style windows give the dining area a medieval character, while the arched, wood-beamed ceiling reminds the guest of the building's humble beginnings.

According to the resident house historian, Francis and Brian could name the spot where they found every piece in the house, from the porcelain kitty on the side table in the lounge to the antique washbowl and vanity in the guest bathroom. Like a living museum, or your eccentric grandmother's place, the Bank House is worth visiting not only for the curated décor but also because

the food is home-cooked (breakfast, lunch, and afternoon tea are served onsite, while dinner is up at the main house) and the setting is absolutely breathtaking. The guest rooms, though decidedly dated, offer spectacular views of the lake, plush carpeted floors, and sinkable soft mattresses—perfect for your return to the Bank House after a nice long walk in the roaming hills. Be sure to ask the staff for a map of the area walks and do not miss the one that leads right from the Bank House left and allows for both a replenishing pint at the pub at the neighboring Howtown Hotel and a dip in the cool lake along the way.

GOSSEL RIDDING   LAKE WINDERMERE, CUMBRIA

*O*NCE UPON A TIME, Gossel Ridding was but a mere fantasy, a pie-in-the-sky dream of its determined builder, George Norman Pattison. The eight-acre hilltop clearing upon which the house now sits, with its massive oak trees and lengthwise view down Lake Windermere, was a favored spot of Pattison's, used predominantly to court women. Thanks to a combination of fate and gumption, Pattison realized his dream in 1908 at the ripe age of fifty, constructing the luxury Arts and Crafts–style estate, having earned his fortune as a successful local builder. Today the estate stands testament to hard work and familial pride: Pattison partnered with his brother, Joseph, and the current owners are their descendants.

The Edwardian Gossel Ridding commands spectacular views over the Troutbeck Valley, through the Langdales, over the bustling village of Windermere, and down the worm-shaped lake. The manse has an unmistakable feeling of sturdiness, perhaps due to the fact that all the materials used to build it come from the surrounding land. Every piece of wood, from the beams to the decorative paneling that covers the interior of the house, hails from oak trees found on the property, while the slate used in the lintels, windowsills, and mullions comes from the area's nearby quarries (some even came from the small, natural quarry in the property's English garden). One of the first things you'll note about the house upon entry is the gorgeous oak paneling and various woodcarvings throughout the ground floor, crafted by the original Pattison brothers and their respective sons from the local oaks. The artisans' names can be found carved into certain panels along the broad staircase.

With such an organic constitution, it's no wonder the house has such a profound effect on its guests and current owners, Teddie and Charlie Pattison, who met and were married onsite. Charlie, a successful film producer, compiled a history of the house and its traditional Arts and Crafts style, while his wife, Teddie, was in charge of updating and outfitting the interiors to today's luxury standards, with plush guest rooms, modern bathrooms, and fashionable, contemporary furniture alongside inherited antiques and original furnishings.

Teddie and Charlie inherited the house in 2006 and began the extensive renovation, which included rewiring, replacing all the windows with double-glazed replicas, adding a new heating system, restoring the woodwork and multiple fireplaces, and remodeling five bathrooms. With the intent of showcasing the house's beautiful antique woodcarvings, Teddie and Charlie chose to replace the damaged furniture with the best of modern design: pieces from B&B Italia, bespoke light fixtures, and natural stone and marble in the bathrooms. The white contemporary style—particularly apparent in the bright and cozy billiard room—creates a lovely, stark contrast that allows the gleaming oak woodwork to shine through without competition.

One of my favorite rooms is the drawing room. Painted a fresh white, the wood paneling and carvings, including the intricate markings on the ceiling, are delightfully mixed in with original furnishings like the Bluthner Leipzig piano (with Ella Fitzgerald sheet music), which bears equally detailed carvings. Other updated furnishings include deep-set B&B Italia armchairs, a particularly alluring, lilac-colored divan in the alcove of the bay windows, and plush white cushions. The ample sunlight in the room, softened by the linen-trimmed sisal rug, invites guests to drape themselves across the round sofa or nestle into the pillows of the armchair and stare out at the lake view.

No vacation estate in England would be complete without its billiard room, and the one at Gossel Ridding, with its ample woodcarvings, is a standout (albeit with a Bose stereo instead of a billiard table). Two long white couches seating up to six each, cushioned side chairs, a quirky white shag rug, and an attractive slate mantel create the desired contrast to the paneling and exposed-beam ceiling, while large cream lampshades hang overhead, reminiscent of the billiard theme. Interestingly, the entire room's paneling comes from one single oak tree from a neighboring farm. The fireplace is the room's undeniable focal point, with a copper chimneypiece, replica fire irons and grate from Hever Castle in Kent, and an antique Charles I fire back. On either side of the fireplace are two carved-wood cupboards, one bearing the initials of the original owner and the other those of his wife, Sally. They are darling emblems in the slate walls that display yet another touch of the house's family pride.

Built to accommodate large groups (the Pattison family was sizable), Gossel Ridding is ideal for house parties with friends or family. The modern, comfy furniture encourages lounging in all the rooms, especially the large, darkened media room, with deep suede sectionals and a massive wide-screen television, appropriately designed by the film-producing owner. The dining room is wonderfully evocative of the house's early twentieth-century origins, with every surface touched by delicate carved details, plus a custom-designed, twelve-person oak table and Gothic-style antique chairs (including one seventeenth-century Hogarth chair with the inscription to prove it). The plaster cornice and beam work were modeled after a seventeenth-century farmhouse. Emphasizing the room's historic feel, Teddie grouped a mass of brass candlesticks in the middle of the table but kept her penchant for contrast by hanging a huge wire globe light as the center chandelier. Last but not least is the welcoming modernized kitchen with its Mercury range, Gaggenau fridge, and Lakeland slate floor with under-floor heating to warm your toes on a winter's morning.

Situated in tourist-haven Windermere, though high above the fray, Gossel Ridding is ideally located for enjoying the tranquility of the lake scenery and the area's charming small shops and cafés. Just a fifteen-minute walk down the road is the town's movie theater, the heralded Beatrix Potter museum, and other perfect rainy-day activities. But when the weather is nice and the afternoon sun is streaming across the daffodil-filled lawn, Gossel Ridding provides the supreme spot to appreciate the dramatic landscape of the Lake District.

ROOMS

In all but one of the seven bedrooms (five double, one twin, and one single), the white-on-white palette with contemporary-style furnishings allows the masterful carved details to stand out. The master bedroom, known to be the best, is also the largest, with wall-to-wall white carpet, two area shag rugs on top, generous curved window, framed by French linen curtains and overlooking the lake, and a dazzling Indian coverlet over the bed. Warm details like the mantel tile with a painted holly leaf motif are pleasing in both summer and winter, but what makes this room special are the elegant Arts and Crafts elements, such as a carved wood armoire, the hidden pocket door to the bathroom, and the curved wood paneling.

My favorite is actually the second-largest bedroom, known as Heliotrope, due to its lavender accents. It has the freshest and most feminine appeal of all the bedrooms in the house, with its romantic fireplace nook accented by violet and white tiles on the mantel and darling inlaid benches upholstered with a floral embroidered silk fabric. One of the few rooms without wood paneling along the walls, Heliotrope features cream-colored raw silk panels with linen curtains, a soft white carpet, and Lucite furnishings by Kartell. Hanging in the center of the room is a vintage chandelier from London's Liberty shop, composed of a group of dagger-shaped crystals that throw the light around, creating a dazzling ambiance in the evening. The room's slate-mullioned windows offer splendid views over the garden (where deer can often be spotted) and down the lake, while the modernized bathroom features natural stone floors, a "sociable shower" (with two showerheads), and an egg-shaped freestanding tub. The sole non-white room, known as the Green Room, features a bright green back wall painted to match the room's aqua and jade mantel tiles and includes a coordinating green throw and pillows. The view is of the hillside, thick with ferns.

All the bedrooms have Hypnos beds with four-hundred-thread-count sheets, L'Occitane products in the bathrooms, and robes from England's White Company. Each room has a shoe basket right outside, meant to deter guests from trekking unseemly mud on the pristine white carpets. There is also a study upstairs, equipped with wireless Internet, a printer, a scanner and a fax machine for those who must work. The Pattisons clearly adore the house and spend a lot of time there, which gives it a feeling of home. They offer guests helpful lists of area attractions, an available concierge service on demand, and the services of affable housekeeper Fay Gorman Hext. For a reassuringly well-appointed and character-laden stay in England's gorgeous Lake District, Gossel Ridding is not only the optimum choice, but a chic one too.

ABOVE The eye-catching exterior of Gossel Ridding OPPOSITE, CLOCKWISE FROM TOP LEFT Fanciful carvings adorn the Arts and Crafts–style house; another example of the family's carving skills; the paneled entryway; the whitewashed drawing room

*T*UCKED BACK IN the moors of the Lake District, not far from the Windermere Golf Club, lies the family-owned country house Gilpin Lodge. Started by John and Christine Cunliffe twenty-one years ago, the twenty-bedroom Relais & Châteaux property has evolved tremendously from its humble 1918 guesthouse beginnings. Today, the Gilpin Lodge is run by the new generation of Cunliffes, Zoe and her husband, Barney, along with Zoe's brother, Ben, an architect. This friendly, personalized small hotel is one of the only remaining privately owned lodges in the Lake District.

Due to its location two miles from Windermere and its lack of actual lake views, the hotel must work extra hard to attract guests. The lodge therefore applies diligent care to its services amenities, from the twenty acres of delightful gardens ideal for afternoon tea or cocktails, to the superb concierge service on hand to book golf lessons, fly-fishing expeditions, chauffeur-driven tours of the lakes, and in-room spa treatments, to the hotel's crown jewel—a highly respected gourmet restaurant and wine cellar. The ground floor offers rambling rooms, multiple lounges, and narrow hallways, typical of the early twentieth century. In response, the owners have created a rather curious configuration and filled the two front drawing rooms with dining tables and used the large back room as a wide, contemporary lounge with plush suede sofas, corner seating areas, and an open archway that leads into the modern wine bar. Given the layout, the house does feel as if it was designed in stages, with each

room's décor marking an obvious departure from the previous one. The fact that there is fluidity to the ground floor, however, is remarkable and likely due to designer Sarah Jane Nielson. The masses of dining tables on either side of the hotel's entryway gives the front entrance (and the arriving guest) a bit of a quirky feel, but instantly informs guests of the hotel's culinary angle.

Fortunately, the house offers ample light with multiple windows, a glass conservatory room (also filled with dining tables), and sliding doors leading to the stone terrace. I found the front left drawing room with its corner table alongside the charming grandfather clock and amid the glittering collections of silver atop various antique dressers and armoires to be the most enjoyable of the dining room options, particularly at breakfast with the morning light streaming in from the windows. The lounge, however, is easily the most comfortable room, capturing guests with its generously sized couches, overstuffed chairs, and Mulberry fabric pillows. The newly designed wine bar offers a contrast to the rest of the house, with an Eastern-influenced décor featuring cream-and-orange-toned wallpapers from Cole & Son and Evans & Brown, offset with natural-colored wicker bar stools, an undulating chandelier from William Yeoward, and contemporary armchairs upholstered in an equally bold russet color. Behind the granite bar lies the glass-encased wine cellar, which is temperature controlled but accessible to all guests interested in browsing or selecting their own bottles. Sets of French

doors open onto the hotel's stone patio, bedecked with umbrella tables overlooking the garden's Asian-inspired ponds and resident llamas in the distance. The bar and patio areas are consistently filled throughout the day and evening with the giddy chatter of guests, many of whom are locals indulging in Gilpin's fine cuisine and notable hospitality. The evening meal's presentation is in keeping with Relais & Châteaux's formal procedure, with menus presented in the lounge over canapés and drinks, followed by lavish, multicourse dinners and lengthy descriptions of each dish from the well-trained wait staff. Dining at Gilpin Lodge is most certainly worthy of a celebratory event.

ROOMS

It appears that Gilpin Lodge has turned its biggest drawback—the lack of lake views—into a source of motivation by focusing considerable energy on the interior design and architectural layout of the guest rooms. The design of the guest rooms was a collaboration between Ben, the architect, who created the six newer garden suites with slanted wood roofs, sliding glass doors, built-in fireplaces, and private decks complete with cedar hot tubs, and Christine, who filled the rooms with bright wallpapers and upholstery in an effort to create an inner sanctuary. One in particular, Haystacks, features a massive, moss-green headboard and alternating wallpapers of reeds and the swirly Cactus Paisley by Neisha Crossland. The color scheme and plush choices of chenille,

PAGE 154 The cozy dining room that was once a parlor OPPOSITE The Asian-inspired lily ponds and dry stone walls of the well-kempt grounds ABOVE The country house exterior and undulating hills in the background

velvet, and silk mimic the fineness of the outside greenery, making the transition from the deck to the indoors almost seamless, while the room's spacious dimensions, high ceiling with skylight, and deliciously deep Duravit are refreshing after a long walk touring the lakes. Don't forget that spa treatments are available in room.

The individually decorated rooms in the main house are divided into three categories: junior suites, master rooms, and classic rooms. Built in 1977, the spacious junior suites have small terraces and charming iron dining sets for spring, some offering split-level layouts. They are all bright and airy, with flat-screen TVs, walk-in showers, and mini-bars equipped with homemade biscuits. The suites come in different color schemes, so it's

best to look online and confirm your preference prior to arrival. My favorites are the more traditional Buttermere and Kentmere, which have ample light, pleasant garden views, and comfortable beds. There is a bit more privacy in Buttermere, with a split-level design, which always makes a room feel bigger. I'm also partial to the room's palette of greens and beiges, with textured wallpapers from Nobilis and Brian Yates, striking fabrics by Zoffany, Colefax & Fowler, and Robert Allan, and contemporary Vincent Sheppard furniture mixed with antique pine pieces.

Among the smaller master and classic rooms, my recommendations are Winster and Crosswaith. Both compensate for their small size with stunning views (especially Winster) and fresh, springy décor, with Jim

Thompson silks, Textura hand-painted wallpaper, curtains from Manuel Canovas, and handmade furniture. Gilpin Lodge also has a bit of a sense of humor and adds signature stuffed animal to various guest rooms, an idea of Zoe's that relays the proprietors' sincere effort to encourage guests to relax.

AUTHOR'S NOTE The lodge's new six-suite Lake House, located a few minutes' drive from the main lodge, on a private lake in one hundred acres of woodland, now provides Gilpin guests the option of exceptional comfort alongside lake views. And with its own spa facility, indoor pool, open-floor-plan rooms, separate kitchens, and secluded location, the Lake House is a fantastic option for groups or families.

ABOVE The artichoke-inspired décor of the Haystacks guest room OPPOSITE, CLOCKWISE FROM TOP LEFT Jim Thompson silks in the Winster Room; a plush, Jim Thompson-covered armchair in Winster; a feast of cushions on the window seat in Cleabarrow Room; another drawing room-cum-dining room

HAYMARKET HOTEL LONDON

$\mathcal{S}$IMPLY PUT, WALKING into the fifty-room Haymarket Hotel, in the heart of London's theater district, brightens your entire day. Whether it is dark and rainy or uncommonly sunny outside, entering the cheerful Haymarket is like stepping out of the thundercloud and into a rainbow. A landmark building designed by John Nash (who also designed Buckingham Palace and Trafalgar Square) in the 1800s, the Haymarket Hotel has enjoyed special distinction in London even before the arrival of style mavens Kit and Tim Kemp.

Not to be outdone by the historic architecture, the Kemps, cofounders of Firmdale, focused their attention on providing inspiring interiors that evoke the grandeur of the building while showcasing their flair for eclectic and modern design. The lobby area features various contemporary artworks, including a massive black-and-white mural by John Virtue, an inlaid pebble mural, and an undulating stainless steel, abyss-like sculpture by Tony Cragg on a pedestal in the center of the room. True to the Kemps' knack for creating an ambiance, the art is offset with eighteenth-century Swedish furniture and elegant recessed lighting. The contrast between London's soot-stained limestone buildings and the bumblebee-yellow furnishings, gray oak floors, and contemporary floral designs feels sincerely uplifting. The spacious ground floor features multiple diversely decorated lounge rooms and galleries, along with Brumus, the hotel's hopping restaurant and bar. The polished oak flooring allows the

sequence of vivid, high-concept interiors to stand out while simultaneously providing some consistency at the rooms' junctions.

Tim handled the architectural side of the remodeling, which was made more challenging by the fact that the Haymarket is listed, while Kit added her signature aesthetic, a "fresh, contemporary English style" to the interior. My favorite ground-floor room, the one that truly made me sigh with content, is the elegant, skylit conservatory with its punchy green and blue leaf fabric and wallpaper from Christopher Farr mixed with beechwood stools from Sempre, dangling globes, and ornate iron griddle lamps. The ethereal forest landscape painting hanging behind the contemporary tufted couch sets a tranquil mood against the hotel's lavish (and delicious) spread for afternoon tea.

In marked contrast, the adjacent, windowless library relies on a smattering of bold, contemporary fabrics from Chelsea Textiles, plum-colored walls, and a brightly woven Turkish carpet and ottoman. The room's requisite bookshelves are filled with antique-bound books, though wedged between the various sets are empty bookbinders lit from within by colorful halogen lights to create the room's very purposeful contrast. Also in the library is a tall wooden chest with an honesty bar, a surprise offering in the middle of downtown London, with copious bottles of wine, Champagne, and various liquors. Guests can enjoy a more secluded drink here than in the hotel's popular bar. In the rear of the ground floor is the vast Shooting Gallery, offering a compelling

backdrop for private events with its gray-toned jungle-theme de Gournay wallpaper, Lucite tables and lamps, and pictures by Oliver Messel of his costume designs for *Antony and Cleopatra*.

Easily one of London's more intriguing subterranean venues, the Haymarket's fifty-five-foot LED-lit pool, bar, and tangential spa is a destination unto itself. Featuring a zinc bar top and gray oak decking, the room was an original (and exclusive) hotspot on Friday nights. Alas, now it is used solely by guests or for private events. Nevertheless the iridescent décor, including the gold-painted leather divans and massive orange, purple, and pink light installation by Martin Richman mounted at the head of the pool continues to evoke a tropical sunset. Given its curious styling (Kit Kemp's Versace moment), with pebble leather bar stools, ornately carved teak chairs, and fiber-optic lighting in the ceiling, the bar is well worth a quick visit for a fruity cocktail. Don't bother with the small gym and one-room spa offering beauty and massage treatments unless you're desperate—the hotel has far more visually arresting elements worthy of exploration.

Brumus is a high-traffic spot for lunch meetings and social dinners, given its central, theater-district location. Its breakfast spread, though, was my own personal highlight. Splendidly laid out on the center oak table are bowls of homemade granola, every type of desirable fruit, four different types of yogurt, daily-made juices, and countless pastries with fresh jams. The signature dish at breakfast is a creative take on high tea called high breakfast, in which everything from eggs Benedict to tiny fruit cups to blueberry popovers and mini-parfaits is stacked upon the customary three-tiered tray. Conceived by the hotel's manager, the high breakfast is the ideal order for the indecisive eater or those particularly fond of sharing. As expected, the room is shockingly bright, with a magenta floral upholstery called Eden by Le Lievre draped on the walls, ceiling, and banquettes, plus oversized Pop Art paintings of breakfast scenes by Peter Rocklin and polka-dot dining chairs by Pierre Frey. The environment is kitschy casual, mixing a dark oak and pewter-topped bar, pewter and mahogany tables, and a life-sized bronze horse. Be sure to sample as much food as possible while at the Haymarket and find time to linger over a meal. Sitting in the festively adorned, naturally lit dining room, particularly in the morning, is a true luxury in the heart of a bustling city.

ROOMS

The Haymarket's guest rooms are located on the historic building's three floors, and each features a unique interior design. Kit and Tim Kemp's hope was that guests would eagerly show off their rooms to one another and thus learn of other rooms' personalized décor. Alas, it's London, and generally visitors are keen to enjoy their room—especially these lavishly designed, spacious ones—in private. Among the largest available in London hotels (due to the building's original and restricted dimensions), the rooms feature dramatic oversized headboards, an

inspiring mixture of modern and antique furniture like shagreen coffee tables and ivory wood-toned pieces, and specially designed lighting, plus a replica of the Haymarket's signature iron mannequin (and logo) fitted into a corner. Given the diversity of the rooms, it's easy to have favorites, though all have distinction and top-of-the-line amenities (including flat-screen TVs, DVD players, and WiFi). The bedrooms are perfectly comfortable for a couple, and their floor-to-ceiling windows (especially on the first floor) offer plenty of light. The one-bedroom suites are my top pick, as the separate drawing rooms are often pleasantly decorated (especially number 112), offering an attractive space for visiting guests or impromptu meetings. One of my favorites is Room 302, a junior suite on the third floor overlooking the fairly tranquil Haymarket Street, with a gorgeous hand printed fabric called Hollyhock Hand by Jean Munro on the headboard. The room's spacious granite bathroom has a separate tub and walk-in rain shower plus a flat-screen TV imbedded into the wall and some of the largest and fluffiest towels in England. I was fortunate enough to stay in Room 111, another instant favorite. With its delightful, turquoise wallpaper from Daniel Croyle, king-sized bed with matching fabric on the headboard, walk-in closet, richly appointed minibar, and, best of all, light-filled corner location, the deluxe room feels so inviting that I didn't leave it for three hours after entry. The one caveat is that by being on the first floor, the noise from the streets is more considerable in this room. I suggest booking either

211 or 311 to ensure the same generous, four-windowed view over Suffolk Street, but with less street noise. The other corner suites are 106, 206, and 306, which offer more light than other rooms, particularly 106, with its floor-length windows.

Throughout my stay, I was delighted by the Haymarket's thoughtful service. Upon arrival guests are greeted with a box of chocolates atop a well-sourced signature pamphlet detailing the surrounding attractions. I was particularly pleased to find the custom-designed "sleep well" mini-spray featuring a soothing blend of lavender, grapefruit, and rosewood oils left on my pillow during turndown (the perfect gift after an evening at smoky Annabelle's) and a full line of Miller and Harris toiletries featuring the signature scent created by Kit Kemp and Lynn Harris of Miller and Harris.

For the complete Kit Kemp immersion, I suggest booking the Haymarket's illustrious and highly exclusive five-bedroom town house. Situated alongside the hotel with its own private entrance, the house is ideal for those seeking ultimate privacy and longer stays; it features its own light-filled drawing room, ground-floor kitchen and dining area, and five spacious double bedrooms with king-sized beds and seating areas.

I can't quite say enough positive things about the guest rooms at the Haymarket, from their cheerful décor to their luxurious amenities and tranquil ambiance. I know that whenever I'm in London, I'll be guaranteed happiness tucked into a plush, strikingly upholstered bed at the Haymarket.

ABOVE One of the junior suites' fanciful fabric headboards and canopies OPPOSITE, CLOCKWISE FROM TOP LEFT The lobby's striking, silver sculpture; the magenta-colored dining room with high breakfast on display; the brightly decorated library makes reading the secondary activity for guest's eyes; the hotel's signature sunset-colored subterranean pool

THE GORING LONDON

QUINTESSENTIALLY ENGLISH, with charming porters dressed in tails and aqua silk ties, the Goring is one of London's most hospitable hideaways in London. Family owned for almost a century, the Goring is that rare species of hotel that offers personal service without forgoing the slightest bit of professionalism, allowing guests to set their desired level of familiarity and accommodating everyone from the chummy regular at the bar to the lunching ladies eager to hit Regent Street. Located near Buckingham, in Victoria, the hotel caters to its local businessperson clientele as much as its guests, with intimate meeting spots like the rich, red-walled bar, the light-filled breakfast hall, or, weather permitting, the lovely veranda overlooking the delightful back garden.

The main lounge, however, is the supreme place to meet, often filled with larger groups settled in the deep velvet couches of the generous corner seating areas. Wonderfully ornate, the lounge features a gold-painted arched ceiling and massive crystal chandelier, bringing an old-world grandeur that seems to promote cocktail drinking no matter the hour. Despite its business-centric crowd, the Goring maintains a strict policy forbidding computer and mobile phone use in the bar or lounge, encouraging guests to converse with one another instead. As a result, the people filling the Goring's sumptuously adorned rooms are actually engaged with one another and their surroundings in a manner that invites the new arrivals to relax in the jovial setting.

With each room more replete with decadent detail than the next, the Goring makes a well-dressed impression. From the harlequin marble floor in the lobby to the silk draped curtains in the dining hall to the multiple arched entryways, the Goring offers a bygone splendor that feels authentic given the British accents wafting around the room. Of course, the staff with pinstriped pants and hot pink ties embroidered with sheep keeps any potential stuffiness firmly at bay. Don't miss the wall of photos over the vintage red tufted couch in the small alcove by the elevators. The pictures showcase the Goring's estimable origins and familial pride, including a portrait of its founder, O. R. Goring, and photos of former staff dating back to 1911, the hotel's second year of business. In fact, the Goring was the first hotel in the world to have private bathrooms and central heating in every room. Not surprisingly, many of the Goring's current staff members have been at the property for more than twenty years, and the hotel, now overseen by Jeremy Goring, is in its fourth generation of family ownership. Today, among the Goring's more amusing signature pieces are the stuffed-sheep footstools that litter the hotel, appearing in various guest rooms and with two rather large ones taking up permanent residence under the lounge's grand piano.

Not to be missed is the Goring's refurbished restaurant, the Dining Room, open for breakfast, lunch, and dinner. With a contemporary design by lauded decorator David Linley and accolades like ITV Tio Pepe prize for Best British Restaurant, the Dining Room provides a welcome contrast to the traditional décor of the bar and lounge. Located further down the hall from the lobby, removed from the other rooms and with a separate entrance, the upscale, seventy-seat eatery serves contemporary English cuisine to a dressed-up crowd. With views over Victoria square, the Dining Room has ribbon-striped high-back chairs, starched percale linen, and crystal obelisk centerpieces. Fortunately, the Goring is just the kind of place you want to dress up for, with personable staff, smiling fellow guests, and classic English dishes like beef Wellington and confit of Lincolnshire pork belly and a double-tiered cheese trolley devoted solely to England's finest.

ROOMS

Of the seventy-one rooms and seven suites, including two Nina Campbell–designed suites and six newly refurbished Gainsborough Silk suites designed by Russell Sage, the favored guest rooms are those located on the second and fourth floors. With wonderful, Cecil Beaton-esque Art Deco furniture and silk wall coverings, the Gainsborough rooms offer an opulent nest after a day out in the city. Cleverly differentiated by their hyperbolic names, the suites at the Goring are worth the extra splurge for their superior décor, natural light, and/or balconies and increased space. The most splendid Silk Room suites are my preference, with French-style floor-length curtains framing bay windows, king-sized beds, and color schemes

PAGE 167 One of The Goring's well-dressed ambassadors ABOVE A rare moment of un-occupation in the living room; a double framed portrait in the mustard-colored breakfast room

The Regency style of the refurbished guest rooms

reminiscent of palaces. The Splendid Connecting Silk Rooms (numbers 58 and 59) are ideal for a traveling family. Both rooms feature handsome silk wallpapers (number 59 with the more pleasing robin's-egg blue), plush seating areas, views, and a balcony (number 58) overlooking the garden. My favorite, number 52, is one of the two Nina Campbell–designed rooms, painted an Oliver Messel mint green. It has a wonderful separate drawing room with an antique-mirrored wall, wood-carved mantel with a decorative gas fireplace, and comfortable beige sofa with aqua, beige, and cream fabric pillows from Nina's collection. The lounge is large enough to hold a spacious writing desk and vintage card table with pewter ashtrays in the corners. Two gilded frames with

female portrait reproductions give the room its Victorian flair, along with floor-length striped silk curtains. Unabashedly feminine, the bedroom's mint-colored toile wallpaper envelops the relatively small space, while clever details like framing the wall-mounted television in gold give the room a pleasant, Gilded Age feel. The marble bathroom has an inviting tub and separate marble shower. Although the room overlooks the front of the hotel and is void of a balcony or the preferable garden views, there is ample natural light and a pleasing layout, especially for someone traveling alone.

The other Nina Campbell–designed suite, room 114, is on the top floor, and although much smaller than number 52, it features the Goring's oft-photographed,

vaulted bathroom. Right in the center, under a circular vaulted ceiling with small picture windows and a Victorian crystal chandelier, sits a resplendent copper tub, simply awaiting your bubble-filled indulgence. The rest of the suite, with its green and maroon fabric, antique-mirrored wall panels, and plush, four-poster bed is pleasant though rather cramped and somewhat lackluster compared with the regal setup for the tub. All of the rooms at the Goring are surprisingly high-tech, given the historic building and its old-world style. Including one-touch lighting systems, flat-screen televisions, air-conditioning, and automatic lights in the bathrooms, the advanced technology may be the only reminder that you are indeed in twenty-first-century London.

OPPOSITE, CLOCKWISE FROM TOP LEFT Number 58's pleasant eggplant and French blue palette; the card room alcove in suite 52; the turret-style bathroom of the Nina Campbell suite 114; room 52's toile-inspired wallpaper ABOVE The dining room's contemporary style

COVENT GARDEN HOTEL LONDON

*L*OCATED IN THE colorful West End, London's throbbing theater district, the fifteen-year-old Covent Garden Hotel commands an ideal position: far enough removed from the main bustle, yet close enough to access the myriad boutiques, brand-name shops, and delightful cafés in the neighboring Covent Garden and Soho neighborhoods. Perhaps the most popular of London's beloved Firmdale Hotels Group (which also includes Charlotte Street, Haymarket Hotel, and the Soho Hotel), Covent Garden is a true emblem of designer and owner Kit Kemp's ability to create a space that is simultaneously a haven and a hot spot. Kemp's signature blend of traditional English style and eclectic, contemporary finds—her modern art collection is one of the most coveted in London—lends a delightful uniqueness to the hotel, making it a must-see for interior design aficionados.

Stepping off the street and proceeding under the cool, gray-striped awning of the entrance and through the black glass doors of the hotel's entrance recalls that delicious, tingling anticipation you felt when you were first admitted to an exclusive spot. The foyer is framed by lush, draped curtains held back with large, roped tassels, setting the stage for a dramatic, theaterlike visual experience. Toward the back of the lobby, alongside the tantalizingly curvaceous marble staircase, is the regal, polished reception desk, which serves as the gateway to the hotel beyond. Despite the lobby's lavish mise-en-scène, guests and visiting diners can be found casually milling about there and in the adjacent

brasserie, chatting on their cell phones or sitting in the lobby's tufted armchairs. The energetic mood is contagious and, given the high quotient of people in the theater business, fabulously entertaining.

A wonderful element of Covent Garden's design is that the common rooms, the lounge and the library, are located on the first floor (that's one floor up in England), providing hotel guests with a serene environment above the hustle of the lobby and a far more private and exclusive place to relax. The magnificent lounge room is alight with Kemp's signature bold juxtaposition of the traditional with the modern, mixing vivid fabrics with oak-paneled walls. In the library more staid décor elements like the large Oriental rug colorfully clash against bright orange and pink side chairs, while two glass-encased model ships are set behind a striking lime, pink, and purple-colored sofa. And while the perfectly fluffed couches in the lounge appear almost too attractive to sit in, answer the impulse and indulge in the sheer pleasure of deflating the sumptuous cushions and nestling into the corner with a good book and spot of tea.

The hotel's sole restaurant, Brasserie Max, is open all day and quite popular with Londoners. The country-style décor, featuring early-twentieth century chandeliers, hot pink and chartreuse fabric curtains, and natural oak floors, gives the spot a friendly, unpretentious feel. The contemporary fare, from hamburgers to simply prepared sea bass, caters to all ages and palates, particularly the summer special: ice-cream sundaes.

Very popular with Americans due to the relaxed atmosphere, top amenities, and family-friendly feel, Covent Garden has been on the radar for travelers for quite some time. However, its groovy location, next to unique London gems like the quirky Neal's Yard, an alleyway with tucked-away cafés and skateboard shops and unconventional décor allow it to retain a hideaway essence .

ROOMS

With each room being entirely distinct from the next, learning the difference between the room types is essential to enjoying your stay. The four room categories—deluxe, queen, luxury, and junior suites—offer not only variance in size but also a striking difference in décor. It is imperative that you ask for a description of the room before booking, as some will be better suited to your taste than others. My favorite rooms (and those most often requested) are 410, 303, 212, and 417. Room 410, the Terrace suite, is the only one in the hotel featuring a small brick patio with potted topiaries and simple teak furnishings. Its interior-facing view keeps it peaceful and quiet. The room features a feminine palette of pinks, oranges, and lilacs, with a striking hot-pink-accented woven carpet and a red background. Gray oak-panel wallpaper offers a note of sophistication. Facing one of the suite's three shuttered windows is an antique writer's desk with brass carved handles and lovely small drawers and cupboards. Room 303, the Loft suite, is the only duplex in the hotel, featuring an elevated bedroom, two

PAGE 172 The mannequin in the guest room: a Kemp specialty ABOVE The alluring library and lounge—a lovely second-floor hideaway
OPPOSITE Kit Kemp's signature blend of bold patterns and stripes works wonders in this small room, one of London's coziest meeting places

bathrooms, and a wonderful alcove library off the generous sitting room. The small arched windows on the first floor give just enough light, though the room is far from bright. The deeply set white linen couches and striped pillows in the lounge are exceedingly comfortable and face a marble fireplace and gorgeous framed prints of empress gown sketches. The bedroom is spacious and open to the lounge below, with an antique mirrored bed that is as luxurious as it is restful. Beware of the air-conditioning system: given that heat goes in one direction, it is imperative to keep the downstairs at a relatively cool temperature to avoid stuffy sleeping conditions upstairs.

Room 417 features the building's original beaming with iron supports and bolts. The French country floral fabric on the headboard and cushioned couch is a pleasant sage color, which is offset nicely by the striped silk bed pillows and crown drapery on the bed frame. The room's slanted dimensions and quirky layout are mitigated by the tall drapery, cushioned window nooks, and well-placed furniture. If you're prone to that nestled feeling that only attic rooms with slanted angles can provide, then this is a wonderfully designed option.

Room 210 has perhaps the most fanciful if not shocking décor scheme. Its bright floral fabric walls, hot-pink felt couch, and

sharp purple suede headboard offer a blast of colors not often found paired together outside a six-year-old girl's bedroom. Nevertheless, the room's generously sized three windows and fabric-covered closet doors give it a cheery disposition that's surprisingly intoxicating. Room 301 is the total contrast to room 210 in that it suits well to the masculine sensibility, with hand-painted coral walls, beige and black ticking-stripe fabric furniture, and horse-and-hound framed prints. Room 212 is a tiny single room, but it has the most pleasing palette with its pretty, deep blues and reds and Guatemalan-looking woven headboard.

OPPOSITE, CLOCKWISE FROM TOP LEFT The duplex loft suite's airy sitting room; room 417's exposed beams give a country-house feel in London; an antique writer's desk; room 212's girly aesthetic ABOVE The "flower-power" guest room

THE ROOKERY LONDON

TUCKED DOWN COBBLED St. Peter's Lane, the Rookery is one of the few remaining guesthouses and bastions of old-world London, clinging to its antiquity with steadfast obstinacy. Located in downtown Clerkenwell, the recently gentrified business area of London, not far from the Barbican and the Tate Modern, the hotel offers a delightful look at the city's architectural history while still allowing guests access to its contemporary culture. Denoted only by a small, overhead swinging sign and gas lantern, the hotel's inconspicuous entrance (save for the impressive, hand-carved door) sets the tone for the secluded haven inside. Constructed from the combination and subsequent extension of eighteenth-century brick buildings, the Rookery is an immersion in period charm, featuring top-to-bottom wood paneling, antique furnishings, and flagstone flooring. More like a gentleman's club than a boutique hotel (the front desk men, dressed in coat and tie, will certainly cause your upper lip to stiffen), the handsome, secluded property is ideal for those intrigued by London's historic, aristocratic glory.

Despite the hotel's antique Georgian interiors, the entire building is wired with high-speed Internet, and the drawing room and library are designated, and often booked, for catered business meetings. Elegantly decorated with polished mahogany antiques, fringed curtains, oil paintings, and stone fireplaces, both rooms offer a classic, traditional space for intimate gatherings. The Rookery's lack of restaurant encourages guests to explore the area eateries, which luckily have become quite good. The concierge is also readily on hand to help book any of London's top spots and arrange speedy transportation. Nevertheless, the hotel does offer twenty-four-hour room service featuring light snacks, available in your room or, more pleasantly, out in the verdant back garden terrace or the charming, aqua-colored conservatory with its working fireplace and potted orchids. A particular treat and well-worn calling card of the hotel is its daily breakfast, served to your room with fresh croissants baked on the premises and steaming tea or coffee, making a long stay in bed a delectable mandate.

ROOMS

Each of the Rookery's thirty-three bedrooms is individually decorated, though all feature magnificent seventeenth-century hand-carved oak beds or Georgian four-posters, with silk pillows and soft throw blankets. The majority of rooms are decorated in traditional Regency shades of yellow, blue, or red with coordinating silk pillows and the occasional embroidered or upholstered furnishing, though some feature mauve, turquoise, or lilac color schemes (which are terrifically English). The furnishings are restored English antiques, polished brightly, and set in carpeted corners underneath framed oil paintings, brass sconces, and chandeliers, ensuring the rooms stay rooted in their historic prominence. Surprisingly the rooms also feature WiFi, air-conditioning, and flat-screen televisions, though that's the extent of the offerings (no coffee or tea or water to speak of). The Rookery's bathrooms are particularly alluring, with original, refurbished fixtures that keep the historic ambiance well intact, while standup showers and Aveda toiletries provide the necessary modernity. Given that the hotel is small and some of the rooms rather tiny, if you have considerable luggage it is well worth upgrading to a suite, simply for storage space alone.

Of the three signature suites, I'm partial to the Rook's Nest, despite my hesitation toward the bed, adorned with corner blackamoors that create odd shadows in the night, and a rather unattractive bedspread. Located in the forty-foot spire, the penthouse duplex features all the requisite (and particularly English) luxury trimmings (including an opulent Victorian tub in the bedroom). I'm particularly fond of the upstairs office with its elegant antique lawyer's desk and cozy corner lounge area with views of St. Paul and the Old Bailey. The Rook's Nest is perfect for a longer stay, when business is an unavoidable element. Beyond the obvious luxury of the suites, I favor two particular rooms (not surprisingly, they are the two featured on the Web site): Simon Michell, a junior suite with gray-painted walls, tall ceilings, and an elevated bathroom, feels light and cozy; and Mary Lane, a superior room with faded golden walls, another carved bed, and tall, silk-framed windows, is comfortably spacious and light throughout the day. In each room is a copy of the Rookery Directory. Leather bound and printed on textured paper with

PAGE 178 An aqua-painted brick wall adds a homey quality to the parlor room
ABOVE The verdant back deck; the hard-to-spot entrance OPPOSITE One of the many antique bathroom fixtures

an antique font, the darling booklet includes an index and old-fashioned profiles on each of the personages mentioned in the hotel, either as names of guest rooms or portraits. It makes for wonderful bath-time reading. Given that the Rookery's rooms are steeped in the building's Dickensian character (some of the guest room names include former local villains and prostitutes), a healthy amount of adventurous spirit is required to enjoy the experience. The bathrooms, while lovely with their Victorian features, are not always the most comfortable, nor are the rooms, with their awkward dimensions; however, what they lack in creature comforts they well make up for in personality, assuring the guest of a distinguished if not rarefied stay in London.

ABOVE The polished signage of the historic property; the rich décor of the ground floor suite
OPPOSITE Carved beds and damask fabric pillows lend an old-world flavor to the historic property

RIGHT BEHIND SOHO SQUARE, tucked into an elegant row of eighteenth-century Georgian houses, sits Hazlitt's, a beloved small hotel that has maintained its historic charm throughout the years. Popular with media and fashion types due to its central location and proximity to Oxford and Charlotte streets, Hazlitt's offers a secluded haven just steps from all the action. The hotel's three interconnected town houses on Frith Street were the former homes of such distinguished Londoners as the 13th Baron of Willoughby, the Duke of Monmouth, and ultimately, William Hazlitt (1778–1830), an essayist for whom the hotel was named. Founded in 1718, Hazlitt's became a visiting house for various notable eighteenth- and nineteenth-century residents whose names now adorn the hotel's thirty-three guest rooms.

Steadfast in maintaining its traditional old-world character, Hazlitt's did little modernizing to the hotel when it opened in 1986, other than add plumbing, electricity, and, more recently, WiFi and satellite television in the rooms. Otherwise the décor is predominantly Georgian, with mahogany antique furnishings, unpretentious silk upholstery, and muted painted walls that allow the various oil paintings to command center stage. Fresh flowers are the only contemporary element in the décor. The concerted effort to preserve the historic essence of the property is indeed its appeal.

From the iconic Georgian-style entrance—with a white column doorframe, black door with iron detail in the window, and center brass mail slot—to the antiques-filled drawing room-cum-lobby with framed oil portraits along the walls, the house engulfs guests in early nineteenth-century style right from the start. The labyrinthine layout of the hotel, due to its architecture of combined buildings, features various winding hallways, three sets of staircases, and multiple back rooms that can get easily confused. Getting from one end of the hotel to the other is daunting given the similarity of the three houses' architecture, including the wonderfully large Georgian windows, which keep the place bright and cheerful. Nevertheless, once you've mastered it, the ground floor quickly becomes like a quirky old house, with sequential drawing rooms, a newly refurbished, peach-colored library featuring guest authors' signed books, an open fireplace, and an honesty bar with whiskey and scotch. The staff, one of the most friendly I've ever encountered, will happily bring light snacks or a spot of tea, or build a fire upon request.

Similar to the Rookery, Hazlitt's offers a private dining room-cum-meeting room with a twelve-person oak dining room table and Georgian-style period sofa. The sofa, one of Hazlitt's most beloved items, is in fact a point of competition among staff members, with all of them hoping to inherit it when the time comes. There is no restaurant, though breakfast, with freshly baked croissants, is served daily, while a competitively priced room-service menu is available all day. Fortunately, Soho is brimming with good restaurants like Arbutus, Barrafino, Quo Vadis, and of course, The Ivy. Given the small size of Hazlitt's and its relative lack of luxury amenities (no gym, private cinema, or flashy bar), the guesthouse is best suited for those who know London and the surrounding area well, who prioritize privacy and charm, and, most of all, who can appreciate the distinctive property's dedication to its preservation and history.

ROOMS

As expected from an old structure, each of the thirty-plus guest rooms at Hazlitt's is unique. I highly recommend choosing a room in the back of the house, away from the street's noise, given that on some nights the neighboring bars can draw lively crowds. Decorated in the Georgian-period style, all of the rooms feature carved oak beds or four-posters, carpeted floors, and silk curtains framing the full-length windows. Some rooms are clearly more comfortable than others, so I recommend booking well in advance, due to their obvious popularity and the smallness of the hotel. I recommend Jonathan Swift, a deluxe room with an Italian marble bathroom, a massive copper showerhead, air-conditioning, a gorgeous eighteenth-century mahogany corner desk, and a tucked-away flat-screen TV with a DVD player. I'm also particularly fond of the chocolate-brown walls, marble fireplace, and romantic crystal chandelier over the foot of the bed. Although the room is rather tight—more than one suitcase can make it feel cramped—the square dimensions and

PAGE 184 The Hazlitt's simple, understated entrance off Soho Square ABOVE Roll-top tubs—a standard in the U.K. and its quintessential properties OPPOSITE An eighteenth-century canopy bed strikes a bold contrast against the turquoise wall

attractive palette of browns and creams make it especially cozy in the winter.

Another favorite room is Madame Dafloz. The jewel-toned aqua and gold silk fabric draped on the bed and upholstered on the pillows, cushioned window seat, and buillon fringe window treatments mixed with the gilded frames and chandelier offer just the right level of opulence. The elegant

mahogany four-poster bed is deceptively comfortable, with soft Egyptian-cotton linens, ample down pillows, and a nighttime duvet. The mounted flat-screen television above the mantel was barely noticeable though appreciated at night when jet lag taunted. I am especially fond of the bathroom, which is shockingly spacious, with a roll-top tub, walk-in shower, shuttered

windows, and the pièce de résistance, an eighteenth-century carved thunderbox toilet. What makes the guest rooms at Hazlitt's so special is they genuinely offer a departure from the outside world, causing guests to submit to the hotel's historic charm and truly indulge in an escape from the norm.

ABOVE The celebrated bed of the Duke of Monmouth guest room

OPPOSITE, CLOCKWISE FROM TOP LEFT The plush velvet couch nestled beneath the windows of guest room Madame Dafloz; the bullion fringe of the curtains in the Madame Dafloz Room; the hidden washroom of one of the classic rooms; the light-filled entryway

HOTELS

HOTEL TRESANTON
27 Lower Castle Road
St. Mawes, Truro, Cornwall
TR2 5DR
TEL: +44 01326 270055
www.tresanton.com
$$$

THE COVE
Lamorna (near Penzance), Cornwall
TR19 6XH
TEL: +44 01736 731411
www.thecovecornwall.com
$$

WHITEHOUSE
Chillington, Devon
TQ7 2JX
TEL: +44 01548 580505
www.whitehousedevon.com
$$

HOTEL ENDSLEIGH
Milton Abbot, Tavistock, Devon
PL19 0PQ
TEL: +44 01822 870000
www.hotelendsleigh.com
$$$

10 GEORGE STREET
10 George Street
York YO1 9QB
TEL: +44 01484 841330
www.10georgestreet.com
$$

WHATLEY MANOR
Easton Grey, Malmesbury, Wiltshire
SN16 0RB
TEL: +44 01666 822888
www.whatleymanor.com
$$$

ROYAL CRESCENT HOTEL
16 Royal Crescent
Bath BA1 2LS
TEL: +44 01225 823333
www.royalcrescent.co.uk
$$$

STON EASTON PARK
Ston Easton (near Bath), Somerset
BA3 4DF
TEL: +44 01761 241631
www.stoneaston.co.uk
$$$

THE RECTORY HOTEL
Crudwell, Malmesbury, Wiltshire
SN16 9EP
TEL: +44 01666 577194
www.therectoryhotel.com
$$

LOWER SLAUGHTER MANOR
Lower Slaughter, Gloucestershire
GL54 2HP
TEL: +44 01451 820456
www.lowerslaughter.co.uk
$$$

BARNSLEY HOUSE
Barnsley, Cirencester
GL7 5EE
TEL: +44 01285 740900
www.barnsleyhouse.com
$$$

LE MANOIR AUX QUAT'SAISONS
Church Road
Great Milton, Oxford
OX44 7PD
TEL: +44 01844 278881
www.manoir.com
$$$$

VINE HOUSE
The Green, Burnham Market, Norfolk
PE31 8HD
TEL: +44 01328 738777
www.hostearms.co.uk
$$

THE PEACOCK AT ROWSLEY
Bakewell Road
Rowsley, Matlock, Debyshire
DE4 2EB
TEL: +44 01629 733518
www.thepeacockatrowsley.com
$$

THE GEORGE IN RYE
98 High Street
Rye, East Susse
TEL: +44 01797 222114
www.thegeorgeinrye.com
$$

$$ moderate
$$$ luxury
$$$$ premiere

SWAN HOUSE
1 Hill Street, Hastings
TN34 3HU
TEL: +44 01424 430014
www.swanhousehastings.co.uk
$$

GRAVETYE MANOR
Vowels Lane, East Grinstead, West Sussex
RH19 4LJ
TEL: +44 01342 810567
www.gravetyemanor.co.uk
$$

HARTWELL HOUSE
Oxford Road, Aylesbury, Buckinghamshire
HP17 8NR
TEL: +44 01296 747444
www.hartwell-house.com
$$

AUGILL CASTLE
Leacetts Lane, Kirkby Stephen, Cumbria
CA17 4DE
TEL: +44 01768 341937
www.stayinacastle.com
$$

YOREBRIDGE HOUSE
Bainbridge, North Yorkshire
DL8 3EE
TEL: +44 01969 652060
www.yorebridgehouse.co.uk
$$

A CORNER OF EDEN
Low Stennerskeugh, Ravenstonedale,
Kirkby Stephen, Cumbria
CA17 4LL
TEL: +44 015396 23370
www.acornerofeden.co.uk
$$

HAMBLETON HALL HOTEL
Hambleton, Oakham,Rutland
LE15 8TH
TEL: +44 01572 756991
www.hambletonhall.com
$$$

SHARROW BAY
COUNTRY HOUSE HOTEL
The Bank House
Sharrow Bay, Lake Ullswater,
Penrith, Cumbria
CA10 2LZ
TEL: +44 01768 486301
www.sharrowbay.co.uk
$$$

GOSSEL RIDDING
Lake Windermere, Cumbria
TEL: +44 07810 091008
www.gosselridding.com
$$$$

GILPIN LODGE
COUNTRY HOUSE HOTEL
Crook Road, Lake Windermere, Cumbria
LA23 3NE
TEL: +44 015394 88818
www.gilpinlodge.co.uk
$$$

HAYMARKET HOTEL
1 Suffolk Place, London
SW1Y 4HX
TEL: +44 0207470 4000
www.firmdale.com
$$$

THE GORING
Beeston Place, London
SW1W OJW
TEL: +44 0207396 9000
www.thegoring.com
$$$

COVENT GARDEN HOTEL
10 Monmouth Street, London
WC2H 9HB
TEL: +44 0207806 1000
www.firmdale.com
$$$

THE ROOKERY
Peter's Lane, Cowcross Street, London
EC1M 6DS
TEL: +44 0207336 0931
www.rookeryhotel.com
$$

HAZLITT'S
6 Frith Street, London
W1D 3JA
TEL: +44 0207434 1771
www.hazlittshotel.com
$$

ABOVE The music room at 40 Winks OPPOSITE The David Tang suite at The Boundary

As always, the hunt for hideaways continues and I am constantly finding fabulous spots that merit inclusion. Two such properties are in East London. The Boundary, a converted Victorian warehouse in Shoreditch, has individually designed suites inspired by notable designers like Mies van der Rohe and one in particular by David Tang called Modern Chinoiserie, which features one of the more beautiful wallpapers to be found in a hotel suite. Also worth noting is the hotel's ground-level cafe, Albion, and adjacent fresh baked food shop, popular with area hipsters and the suits who support them. The second spot, 40 Winks, is a hideaway that eschews

today's hospitality norms by reintroducing the very British, guesthouse-stay where the owner remains in-house. The eighteenth-century Queen-Anne townhouse is owned and managed by the lauded designer David Carter, whose vamped, glamourpuss-style decor beckons fashionistas and art director-types eager for a taste of something a bit more cultivated than the norm. Just two bedrooms and one bath, the house is best appreciated when rented entirely, assuring the guest of delicious one-on-one time with the charming owner and the undisturbed experience of staying in one of London's most fantastical homes-away-from-home.

ACKNOWLEDGMENTS

ᴅᴇsᴘɪᴛᴇ ᴛʜɪs ʙᴇɪɴɢ my third installment in the Hideaways series and the presumption that I've gotten more streamlined in my process, just like its predecessors, the completion of this book would never be possible without the hard work of so many others. As always, I am forever indebted to each of the Hideaway properties that I discovered and the people who own and manage them. It was my sincere pleasure to visit each spot and I owe whatever success of the book to their generous involvement.

This book, simply put, would not look half as enticing if it weren't for the magnificent Tim Clinch. My deepest gratitude goes to Tim for his stupendous work, flawless driving skills and guidance throughout the exhausting adventure of 'An American in England'. May the joy of a pint of Harveys and England as the perennial victor of the Ashes, be with you always. I also want to thank Tim's agent, Karen Howes of Interior Archive, for ensuring the right man for the job and Olga Polizzi for her warm introduction.

Next, I'd like to thank my lovely editor Kathleen Jayes and her phenomenal counterpart, Ellen Cohen who helped steer me through a deadline alongside pregnancy and the sequential late hours of newborn care. Without their gentle prodding and timely reminders, this book may never have been. I'm also particularly beholden to Ellen's fastidious nature and dedication to the book's success along with Sara Stemen's beautiful design and boundless patience. I'd also like to thank the Rizzoli Publicity department, Pam Sommers and Nicki Clendening especially, for their continual efforts of the Hideaways series. Another large thank you to Rizzoli publisher, Charles Miers who continues to grant me the delicious freedom of selecting properties according to my own sensibilities, even when the host country is his own.

And last, I'd like to thank my husband, Friso, my parents; Bob and Liz Nolan, my in-laws; Nickel and Gusta van Reesema, siblings; Bud and Lilly, my friends and colleagues, particularly Catherine Fiederowicz, whose London pad was the starting point to the whole adventure, and most of all, my baby boy, Winslow, to whom I dedicate this book. Without their support plus Winn's coos of encouragement, this book simply wouldn't be.

A vintage-inspired bicycle
at Whatley Manor

First published in the United States of America in 2011
by Rizzoli International Publications, Inc.
300 Park Avenue South, New York, NY 10010
www.rizzoliusa.com

DESIGNED BY Sara E. Stemen
EDITOR: Kathleen Jayes
PROJECT MANAGER: Ellen R. Cohen

ISBN: 978-0-8478-3544-7
Library of Congress Control Number: 2010941558

PRINTED IN CHINA

2011 2012 2013 2014 / 10 9 8 7 6 5 4 3 2 1